# CRYSTALS

## FOR BEGINNERS

A Practical Guide to Using Healing Crystals and Stones

*By*
Abigail Welsh & Edson Keenan

© **Copyright 2020 - All rights reserved.**

The content contained within this book may not be reproduced, duplicated or transmitted without direct written permission from the author or the publisher.

Under no circumstances will any blame or legal responsibility be held against the publisher, or author, for any damages, reparation, or monetary loss due to the information contained within this book. Either directly or indirectly.

Legal Notice:

This book is copyright protected. This book is only for personal use. You cannot amend, distribute, sell, use, quote or paraphrase any part, or the content within this book, without the consent of the author or publisher.

Disclaimer Notice:

Please note the information contained within this document is for educational and entertainment purposes only. All effort has been executed to present accurate, up to date, and reliable, complete information. No warranties of any kind are declared or implied. Readers acknowledge that the author is not engaging in the rendering of legal, financial, medical or professional advice. The content within this book has been derived from various sources. Please consult a licensed professional before attempting any techniques outlined in this book.

# CRYSTALS FOR BEGINNERS

By reading this document, the reader agrees that under no circumstances is the author responsible for any losses, direct or indirect, which are incurred as a result of the use of information contained within this document, including, but not limited to, — errors, omissions, or inaccuracies.

# CRYSTALS FOR BEGINNERS

## Table of Contents

Introduction ................................................................................... V

Chapter One - Why Use Healing Crystals? ..................................... 1

Chapter Two - Best Crystals To Heal Your Emotions ............. 27

Chapter Three - Recommended Crystals For Beginners ....... 74

Chapter Four - How To Use Healing Crystals ........................... 88

Chapter Five - Tips To Maximize Your Healing Crystals .... 118

Final Words .............................................................................. 133

# INTRODUCTION

Healing crystals have had a resurgence in popularity recently. The internet has helped this to a large degree, as it has made it easier to find out information on this fascinating topic. The interest in using healing crystals for emotional wellbeing has caught on with celebrities, fashion designers, and adherents of New Age lifestyles. Crystals have taken over Etsy, the online marketplace that specializes in handcrafted, alternative, and custom-made items and gifts. In fact, because Etsy has found them such a fast-selling product, it's been difficult for them to retain any stock. Crystals are very popular with those people who like "mystic beauty," a style of fashion that mixes spirituality with beauty. Examples of mystic beauty products are necklaces or dresses which use healing crystals as part of the design.

Healing crystals first came to the wider public's attention in the 1970s. At that time, what we'd now call New Age philosophies were still developing out of the hectic youth culture experimentation of the 1960s. This made it very easy for people to dismiss these crystals as a bunch of nonsense, or even see them in a sinister light. The late 1960s had seen the optimism of the Summer of Love when young people on America's West Coast converged in attempts to find new spiritual and cultural paths but had then witnessed such ideals perverted by the appalling violence of the Manson "family." It became very easy to disregard anything derived from such sources as escapist or dangerous. The exploration of spirituality and alternative forms of healing slowly faded as the 1970s progressed. By the time the 1980s came around, cultural values had moved fully from spirituality and emotional exploration. By then, the focus was on trickle-down economics and the new war on drugs. Healing crystals faded from the popular consciousness at this time, though there were those who continued to teach of them and sing their praises.

As we've progressed into our modern, technologically connected age, there has been a return to the spirituality of this earlier period. Despite being more connected than ever before, people are experiencing greater loneliness and anxiety than was common in the past. Our brains evolved throughout history in order to allow us to function as communities and tribes. We just aren't supposed to be exposed to so much marketing and advertising. We're not even very good at maintaining a social circle of more than 150 people, including family, friends, neighbors, and coworkers. This modern malaise is responsible for a return to spirituality, and with it has come a reawakening of interest in healing crystals.

Despite being included under the umbrella title of New Age, the use of healing crystals is said to go back throughout most of human history. It is safe to say that we have always found crystals compelling. They were used to show class and rank or to accentuate beauty. As we developed better sciences, we discovered that crystals could be used in electronics and other modern inventions. The use of crystals in science shows us that there are definitely practical uses and purposes that they can be put towards. Most people readily accept that. But when you start to mention crystal healing, you often end up with these same people largely dismissing the idea. These individuals often view crystal healing as a nonsense belief that isn't grounded in science. Or, they might see such ideas as a sign of occult influence, that dark, possibly Satanic, forces are attempting to do harm to the world. This second belief we can dismiss out of hand. There is nothing occult about using healing crystals. There is no dark energy, no evil presence, no Satanic masterplan. But that comment about science brings up an intriguing thread to explore.

# CRYSTALS FOR BEGINNERS

If you don't believe that crystals have mythic properties that allow for healing, then I am not about to try to change your mind. However, if you argue that there is no science behind using healing crystals, then I would suggest that is taking far too hasty a view. It is perfectly true that science does not point towards a clear result that states, "These crystals have healing properties, and we should study them more." But science doesn't need to look at healing crystals *directly* to show how they do have power. The findings that tell us the most about healing crystals actually come from drug testing.

When you test a new drug, you don't just give it out to somebody and watch the results. Instead, you gather together a few test groups. You give the new medication to one group, and you give a placebo to the other group. This is known as double-blind testing. The sign that a drug genuinely has potency is when the results show that the group that received it has a higher success rate than those that didn't. But those that didn't still often show the effects of the drug, despite not taking it. This is called the placebo effect, and it ties directly into our use of crystals.

The placebo effect is in and of itself a truly mind-boggling phenomenon. If we are told that we have taken a drug, we expect that drug to begin to work. This expectation or belief then fuels a physical or mental change within our bodies. There was an old prank in my high school where people would pretend to dose others with LSD. They would tell them that they slipped it into their drinks or food. The unfortunate victim would then trip out, and often, they were sent to the nurse's office. Yet there was never any LSD present; it was entirely a lie told for the prank. But the person who was tricked fully believed it, and they would swear that they were hallucinating. The reason this is so fascinating to me is that it demonstrates how our brains have the ability to change how our reality works based on what we believe to be true about reality. Therefore, it can be argued, healing crystals work so long as you believe in them.

You might counter that the placebo effect only shows us that healing crystals don't work at all, that they aren't real. But if the placebo effect can completely alter the lived experience of a person, then how is that anything but real? All we are as we go through this life is our consciousness, so if that can be altered, then reality itself is alterable. Further findings in this direction come from the scientific study of the brain and how it is affected by religion. Scientific research has indicated that people who believe in God experience less pain when they pray. A religious person may ascribe this to divine intervention, though a scientific-minded person would argue for a placebo effect. But, if it is a placebo effect, does this mean that God isn't real?

In a way, healing crystals are the same. If you believe in them, then they are going to work. If you do not believe in them, then they are unlikely to work for you. But if you are on the fence, then it can go either way. However, we can make the active choice to believe in the healing properties of these crystals. When we do this, we ensure that they work for us because we have deemed that reality to be so.

My goal is this book will not be to convince you one way or another that these crystals really work. I am quite sure that they do, and I believe that you agree with me, or you will do so before too long. My goal, however, is to introduce you to the many reasons why people use healing crystals. From there, we will explore the best crystals for healing our emotions and what crystals are most appropriate for beginners. With a solid understanding of all these moving parts, we'll turn our attention to the various ways that we can use healing crystals in our lives and then close out on tips for improving your healing crystal experience. By the time we finish, it is my hope that you will have a deep understanding and appreciation for these remarkable and powerful tools.

# CHAPTER ONE

# WHY USE HEALING CRYSTALS?

The title of this chapter asks an important question. Just exactly why is it any of us should be worrying about or using healing crystals? The answer to this particular question is not exactly hard to answer. In fact, you'll find that there are many different answers to this question plastered all over the internet. But the plethora of answers also brings with it a problem: Which are right?

Unfortunately, this isn't one of those issues which has a single simple answer. There is no one reason to use healing crystals. There are dozens upon dozens. Some of these uses seem to go together quite well and make it easy to see the way they interact with each other. But then there are those answers which seemingly contradict other answers. If you believe that there is one solid answer as to why you should use healing crystals, then you are going to wind up somewhat frustrated with the whole ordeal.

In order to give this question enough room to be properly answered, I have collected together many of the different reasons people use healing crystals. These range from seeking balance and calming the emotions to stepping out of the electromagnetic field, finding pain relief, romance, or even detoxifying your home. You'll notice that these range from the purely psychological to the entirely mystical. I'd like to give you a full understanding of the topic, rather than one that simply dismisses or wholly embraces the mystical realm. Each of us has our own spiritual beliefs and ideals. Rather than try to convince you of a spiritual concept, this approach will let you investigate it for yourself to decide if crystal healing is right for you.

## Getting in Touch With Your Emotions

Many of us go through life as a slave to our emotions. If we are happy, then we think that life is wonderful, but when we're sad or anxious, we think that life is horrible, that it only wants to hurt us and that it never did anything good for anyone. If you believe in chakras, then you may see this as a sign that your chakras are clogged up, but most people don't have this disconnection from their own emotional experience. Instead of seeing their emotions as something that *happens* to them, they see emotions as an intrinsic part of themselves. We all tend to do this, to over-identify with our emotions instead of regarding them as transient phenomena. Getting lost in our emotions can be very scary, but healing crystals can help us out a lot in this area.

Different crystals have different purposes. There are those that help with romance, those that help with pain, some that help to calm us, and some that improve our concentration. We'll be looking at these in more depth throughout the book, but the range of uses points towards our emotional experiences. How can we be calm if we are lost in our emotions? As we'll see, we can turn to a healing crystal.

Regardless of how you use your crystals (which we cover in depth in chapter four), one of the powerful things about them is the way that they take on meanings of their own. For example, we use amethyst to help us deal with our anxiety or sadness. If we find that we are overly irritable, then we'll use some jade. If we have too much stress, we can use the gorgeous moonstone to help us let it go. These are just a few of the available crystals we use for emotional purposes, but how do they help us?

We'll be using the word intention a lot throughout the book. For our purposes right now, an intention is simply the purpose that we intend our crystals to serve. So, if you are stressed, then you would take a moonstone and set the intention as stress relief. As you gather more crystals around you, you'll come to have one or two each for most of your emotions that you need help dealing with. When you feel the negative emotion, you then turn to your healing crystals rather than get lost in it. Whether it is the crystal itself or the intention that you set, which helps you to deal with the feeling, the result is the same. You create a space between yourself and your emotional experience and then use crystals to alter and change it.

Practicing with healing crystals is a fantastic way to learn more about your own emotions. They also offer a wonderful way of getting in touch with your reactions and responses. You need first to identify that you are upset before you can turn to your healing crystals to help you manage it. This act of identifying your emotional experience is one of the most effective ways of understanding your own emotions and thus being able to conquer them.

**Seek Balance**

We mentioned chakras in the last section, so let's continue with them for a moment. If you believe in chakras, then you know that they are situated throughout your body, and each one acts almost like a gate. If they are open, then healing energy can flow through them. When your chakras are open, you have a great sense of peacefulness and contentment. But problems start to occur when they get closed or blocked up. In fact, if you believe in their significance, most of the emotional and mental problems that we experience are explained through chakras

Everything in the world is made up of frequencies, primarily electromagnetic, and crystals are no different here. However, different crystals have a different frequency, and this is what makes them better or worse for a particular use. We are said to have seven different chakras, and each of these reacts to a different frequency. We might have problems in our lower chakra and find that we can't find romance or sexual fulfillment. Or we might have a problem with our throat chakra and find that we never speak up for ourselves, ask the questions we need to know, or speak in a manner that touches the depths of our inner being. When this is the case, we can turn to different crystals. For example, we might wear a necklace with lapis lazuli in it so we can unblock our throat chakra.

If you are finding that you feel like you are out of balance in your life and in your mind, then you may want to consider exploring your chakras. A healing crystal could help you in this matter so that you can live your life as the most activated and honest version of yourself possible.

**Romance and Sexual Energy**

Both romance and sexual energy have chakras assigned to them. Romance is located in the heart, while sexual energy or potency is found in the lower regions just above the genitals. These are two of the spaces which are said to get blocked up the most often. When we are unlucky in love, we can often convince ourselves that we were meant to be alone or that our loneliness is a sign of our worthlessness. There is nothing wrong with a relationship ending or a date going poorly; this is simply the risk involved in any interpersonal relationship. But when we convince ourselves that our love life is a sign of something wrong with us, we clog up our chakras. Or, if you don't believe in chakras, you might interpret this as the way we can get lost in our thoughts, and allow our negativity to spiral out and affect our lives.

One use for healing crystals is to help repair this damage in our hearts. To help us deal with matters of romance, we use a crystal with a pink, orange, or red color. This color alone connects it to the same emotional sphere as love, and this helps us to fuse our intentions into the crystal and our minds. We may choose to wear a low-hanging necklace so that we can keep our healing crystal over our hearts and allow its vibrational frequencies to be closest to our love chakra.

Another issue that we often face is thinking that we are sexually repulsive or too unqualified to pleasure another being. While we might not have much experience, there is no reason that we should feel this way. When two people come together, they need to discover each other's bodies themselves to learn how they work. This is a process filled with errors and mistakes and (hopefully) laughter and love. But we live in a society that tells us how well we should perform, when we should have sex, how long we should be having it for, and all sorts of other weird messages that leads to confusion and can result in us getting bewildered and lost. Rather than live in the experience and enjoy it for what it is, we burden ourselves with anxiety and worries and nervousness, and these can greatly reduce how pleasurable the experience is for both parties.

By infusing a healing crystal with sexual energy, we can break free from the messages we have been told, and, instead, get back in touch with the act itself. You may want to meditate with your crystal before performing, or you may want to wear it on a bracelet or something similar. By setting your intention ahead of time, connecting with this crystal becomes a way of tapping into the limitless libido inside of us all.

It should be noted that healing crystals used for matters of love don't just refer to the type of romantic love between two people. These crystals can also be a great way to get in touch and rediscover a love for yourself. If you are having a hard time accepting who you are or if you don't love yourself yet, then a healing crystal with an intention of love might be exactly what you need.

**Improve Psychic Powers**

You don't need to be a psychic to get benefits from using healing crystals. This is a common myth that is common around many of the practices that have come to be known as New Age. The perfect example of this is tarot cards, as they are one of the most widely known of these practices. But just like tarot cards, healing crystals are more often used for the psychological benefits that they provide rather than psychic ones. Just like tarot cards, healing crystals can be used for psychic purposes, though this is not their most common use. It is like using a spoon as a fork, it can do what you want, but it wasn't intended for this purpose.

Those with psychic powers may use amethyst or apophyllite to activate and strengthen their third eye, that psychic eye that exists inside the forehead and the brain. The crystals are given the intention of improving your psychic abilities, and then they are typically worn as part of a decorative headband, or they are placed on the forehead during meditation. The vibrations from these crystals help to open up and clear out the third eye so that your psychic visions will be more powerful.

**Improve Your Skin**

While some of us aren't especially bothered, most of us want to have beautiful and healthy-looking skin that is clear from blemishes and other unattractive features. The populations of affluent countries spend millions upon millions of dollars on skincare products, not just every year but every single quarter. New products come out all the time with the latest scientifically formulated mixture to ensure that your skin looks wonderful. But, instead of turning to these endlessly new creations, perhaps we could benefit from turning towards something a little bit older. It has been this idea that has driven the market of healing crystals used in skincare products.

There have been quite a few products of late that use small pieces of crystal to ensure beautiful skin. One example is the Gemstone Organic Rose Quartz Creme, which uses rose quartz as well as smoky quartz and kunzite. Another product is the Tracie Martyn Complexion Savior, which includes a little bit of malachite. Of course, it should be clear that these use healing crystals as part of their overall product and not as the product itself. This brings into question whether or not the crystals have anything to do with improving the skin at all. It could just be that the pharmaceutical ingredients do all the work.

In that case, what about a face roller that uses jade? These have been around for quite some time, and they are known to help reduce the puffy appearance of skin. Not only that, but they leave a noticeable shine to the skin that suggests that they help bring the natural oils to the surface. This is further backed up by the fact that jade rollers help the skin to absorb creams and other rub-on products. That's made possible by the way jade helps to open the pores of the skin. So next time you are thinking about purchasing some facial cream or other skincare products, consider adding healing crystals to your routine.

## Help Plants Grow

This is one of the many uses that healing crystals have around the house. Some people like to bring healing crystals into the home for decorative purposes, but others use them in a more thoughtful manner (such as for feng shui, covered next). This particular use is one that stands outside of any science that I know of, including that of the placebo effect. Simply put, plants don't have the neurological component necessary for the placebo effect to work. It may be that adding crystals to a plant provokes the placebo effect in the owner, as they see the crystal as doing the work rather than the plant's environment and biology. But when looking for more information on this particular use, it becomes clear that it is tightly tied to psychic explanations.

There is a tendency to think of psychics as having the ability to see into the future or perceive the possible threads of fate as they are weaved together. This is most obvious in jokes made at the expense of psychics such as "If you're psychic, then you should know who's calling." But what these miss is that a psychic isn't necessarily able to see into the future, so much as they work from and through emotions, intuition, and other unseen elements of understanding. One of the things that is often reported is that psychics have a strong connection to nature, or they have an intuitive sense as to the needs of Mother Nature. It is this connection that leads us to the use of healing crystals in raising plants.

Crystals are added to the soil or to the container housing the plant. The plant's vibrational frequencies should be in the same range as the crystal. This needs to be discovered intuitively, and some psychics suggest asking your plants which crystals they want to use. Add the crystal and watch as the plant begins to thrive.

**Aid in Feng Shui**

Chakras are one of the ways that we explain and understand the emotional and spiritual experiences that we are having as we go about our lives. They play on the unseen energies that affect and move us all. Each of us is a world unto ourselves, and this means that we bring our energies with us no matter where we go. But there is also environmental energy; unseen forces which lend power to the places we occupy. If you have ever walked into a room and immediately felt a negative energy, then you know first-hand the way that locations can take on and store their own emotional and intangible vibrational energy.

One way that we cleanse and balance these environmental energies is through the use of feng shui. Rather than living at odds with the environmental energy around us, feng shui gives us a way of smoothing out our experience so that the energy of the environment and the energy that we bring can coexist without clashing. Feng shui practices range from the way you position furniture to how often you clean your windows, as well as what objects you bring into the house. Some of the objects that we can use to increase our feng shui are healing crystals.

These stones represent a form of energy taken from the earth. They are energy collected into a physical form that you can then use with care and consideration to assist in your life and your feng shui. Just as these crystals can be used to balance our emotions, they can be used to help us balance the energies of our home. But to this end, it is important that we keep in mind that each crystal has a different purpose and power. It doesn't help our feng shui out if all we do is place crystals around the house in a haphazard and unconsidered manner. If you were placing heaters in your house, you wouldn't just toss them anywhere. You would consider each room and where the best location to put them is and how much heat you need in a particular space. Healing crystals should be used in this manner, considered and placed carefully to achieve an effect rather than left to the chaos of indifference.

The most commonly used crystal in feng shui is the jade crystal. This crystal is said to bring good luck to the owner and makes the home into a luckier space. It also represents the possibility of new beginnings, so it is a particularly great crystal to begin with, in the sense of starting to use crystals as a beginning in and of itself. Jade is also said to bring fortune into the household, and so it is commonly paired with the money bonsai as a gift since both are meant to bring riches. Also used often is clear quartz, which helps to remove the negative energies from around the home. Rose quartz is also quite popular since it represents love. If you are married, then rose quartz is used to help strengthen the relationship and create a loving energy in the home. Remember that these are just a few examples of how healing crystals are used in feng shui, I'm sure you'll discover plenty more yourself.

## Pain Relief

Pain can cripple us and steal away our lives. Or, at least, it can make it feel that way. If you experience chronic pain, then you know first-hand how debilitating it can be. You might have a thousand things you need to get done, but if you're in too much pain, then there's no way you're going to get out of bed. If you experience anything that brings a lot of pain into your reality, then you've probably looked for ways to treat it. While modern medicine has achieved wonders in this field, there is still a lot of work that needs to be done. I can't begin to tell you how many people I've met that have been prescribed opiates despite not wanting them. It seems that our main way of dealing with pain is through dangerously addictive chemical concoctions. I don't want to suggest that these have no value, but they do have many negative side-effects, and this puts many people off using them.

Healing crystals offer us another way of dealing with our pain, and there are tons of people who swear by them. Whether it was their natural frequencies that helped out or it was the placebo effect, the fact of the matter is that many people have found pain relief through using crystals. They are not the kind of thing that would be recommended by doctors, but they can help. Rather than claim them to be better or worse than medication, please make sure you seek out a professional medical opinion in conjunction with their use rather than relying solely on the crystals. With that said, let's take a quick look at some of the crystals that people use to take their lives back from pain.

Amethyst is often called the master healer, and it is considered to be the most effective crystal in treating pain. It has a very high frequency of vibration that makes it appropriate for treatment of pains such as arthritis or headaches. It is also used to treat stress. Cortisol, the stress hormone, can make pain worse, so this is doubly beneficial. Lapis lazuli is also recommended for pain relief, though it only has minor healing properties that make it best for smaller pains. What lapis lazuli has going for it is the fact that it helps to strengthen the mind, and this can make us better at withstanding and putting up with pain. Hematite is used to help with the flow of blood through the body, and it is worn to reduce blood pressure and other issues that can make your veins feel like they are filled with fire. Rose quartz is used in the treatment of skin, not only as a cosmetic, but also to reduce the pain from burns and inflammatory issues. If you've got a sunburn, use a little rose quartz along with your aloe vera to help lower the level of pain overall.

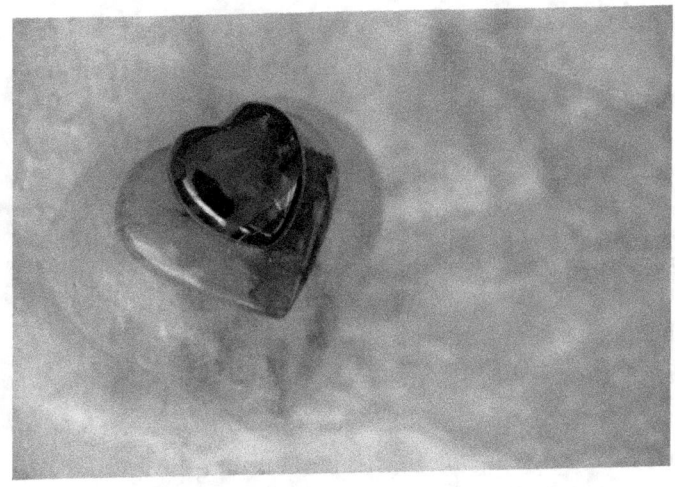

**Increase Your Happiness**

We already talked about how healing crystals can help you to get in touch with your emotions. This same feature has a bi-product of helping you to understand your own happiness in a much fuller sense. But this isn't the only way in which healing crystals improve and increase our happiness. There are many different crystals that are said to have healing powers, and we'll briefly glance at those here, but, first, there is a more mundane consideration we need to take into account. Simply put: crystals are attractive.

One of the reasons that crystals became so popular was because of their gorgeous looks. They can have bold bright colors, or they could be clear or even entirely dark. Some shine, others let light pass through them. They all have different textures and feelings, and these can make them quite enjoyable to hold in your hand. The beautiful nature of these crystals tends to spark reflection and to bring the mind into a pleasant state as you consider their beauty. One of the best things we can do for our happiness is take in beautiful things such as nature or art, and crystals are another of these beautiful objects we can use to improve our sense of wellbeing.

Moving on from crystals as a whole, we find that there are many different healing crystals that are said to have ties to the emotional sphere of happiness. The amazonite is said to bring joy through the way it helps us discover and listen to our inner thoughts and feelings. We each have an inner truth, a way that we want to live. This isn't the same as an ambition like, "I want to be a successful writer or actor." Instead, this is more like, "I want to be a good person and to bring positivity to those around me." This is a deeper truth. Unfortunately, we often have a hard time connecting to such truths, and thus we live our lives as we are told we should and not as we genuinely want to deep inside. Amazonite can help us to connect to this truth. In doing so, it helps us to live more honestly and fully and to appreciate those around us, as well as ourselves.

Citrine is a beautiful, bright yellow crystal. If we look at citrine, it is hard not to think of the sun and the brightness of day, or the warm feeling that comes from bathing in its rays. This stone brings a feeling of being carefree and makes us more likely to take actions that put us outside of our comfort zone. While this may sound - pardon the pun - uncomfortable, psychologists have discovered that we are at our happiest when we are trying new things and pushing ourselves to achieve more.

Tiger's eye is another crystal with connotations of nature and the sun. Its tiger-striped colors bring in lots of browns as well, and this evokes a lovely feeling of nature, of the forests and trees that provide us with our oxygen and thus our ability to live in the first place. This helps us to tap into that primal center inside of us all so that we can find strength and courage to take on whatever life throws at us.

You might be noticing a pattern with these three crystals. While some are said to bring happiness directly, many crystals don't actually do this. What they do is to help bring balance across our whole so that we can more easily find happiness. They help us to reduce our stress so that we can live happier. They help us to push outside of our familiar routines so that we can be more inventive and energetic. They help us to tap into our internal strength so that we can discover more about ourselves. All these are avenues to find happier lives. They don't directly affect happiness, but they affect the factors that help contribute to happiness in a positive way.

**Tap Into Calmness**

One of the things that has already begun to crop up frequently throughout this book is the way that our modern world isn't designed to facilitate our emotional needs. Nowhere is this more clear than when we look at the idea of calmness. Have you noticed how everything seems to happen faster and faster these days? We have a 24/7 news cycle, and our social media feeds never ever end; they just scroll on forever. Commercials are edited to overload our senses, and we're constantly fighting traffic jams, balancing our finances, and trying to get promoted. All of this tells us to go, go, go, but it doesn't consider what this is doing to our psyches. Our constant need to push forward and keep moving, keep aiming for what's next, keep up with the news, and stay active online all cause us lots of stress. We don't always notice that we have this stress because we're so bombarded with it that we've come to think it is normal.

But then it comes time for bed, and we find ourselves unable to sleep. We're restless. We've been told to go faster and faster, to do more and more, to take in more information. But we're never told to relax and calm down, and take time away to get back in touch with ourselves, to seek out a piece of calm within us. This message has been so readily ignored that many of us think that calmness is a bad thing.

But if we want to live a healthy life, then we need to find a calm center in ourselves. This will lower our anxiety, improve our happiness, and increase our life expectancies. But with so many of us unsure of how to go about it, it can be hard to achieve. Thankfully, there are healing crystals that can help us here.

Amethyst, hematite, and moonstone are just three types of healing crystals that help to create a sense of calm. Their energies are very mild. This doesn't mean that they aren't potent, but they help us in a way that isn't explosive or over the top. They do the exact opposite; they soothe us instead of stimulating us. These calming energies can be felt when worn as jewelry, but the most effective approach is to combine calming crystals with meditation or even a bath. These activities already help to promote a sense of calm that grows exponentially when combined with the use of a healing crystal picked and imbued for this purpose.

**Protection from Negative Energies**

One of the ways that we protect ourselves from negative energies is by seeking understanding and balance in our emotional realm. Another way is to use feng shui to make our living environment into a more relaxed and positive place. But these are just two ways in which we bring positivity into our lives. To use a stretched metaphor, this kind of protection is like purchasing a gun. It can bring with it a sense of protection, but it doesn't do anything to prevent intruders. Likewise, when we balance our emotions or use feng shui, we are increasing our happiness, but we aren't preventing the negative from entering our lives. To complete the metaphor, we don't need a gun. We need a fence.

We built a fence up around our happiness, and this protects us from negativity. We might still encounter negativity in our lives, but our fence keeps it at a distance. We aren't opening our doors and inviting it in. We can see it, recognize it for what it is, and then go back inside and continue to be content. Since we're talking about happiness and negativity, there are no real fences. But we can use healing crystals to give us an assist in this manner.

Some healing crystals are said to be used for protection such as fire agata, black obsidian, or fluorite. Adding these stones to your home, or to your jewelry, can help to give you this protection. Whether the stones do it themselves, or they function on the placebo effect again, the result is the same. You become more aware of the way that you interact with negativity, and this helps you to distance yourself from it. Knowing that you are protected, you can see the negativity without looking through the eyes of fear.

If you want the most protection possible, then a bracelet or necklace with multiple crystals is the way to go. But don't just use stones that are meant for protection. Instead, use a protection stone and then a happiness stone, another protection stone, and then a stone for health. By combining these, you create a piece of jewelry that not only protects you from negativity, but it actively invites positivity into your life as well.

## Chapter Summary

- There are many reasons why people use healing crystals in their lives. No one reason is better or worse than another, as these are very personal and determined by the individual's relationship to their crystals.

- We are often controlled by our emotions, but healing crystals are one of the ways we can take control back. By understanding our emotions enough to pick the right crystals to improve them, we get more in touch with ourselves.

- Our chakras often get clogged up and unaligned. This can bring great discomfort to our lives, but these blockages can be cleaned away through the use of healing crystals that help us to align our chakras and live more fully.

- While there are healing crystals for our emotions such as happiness or anger, there are also healing crystals that help us to invite more love into our lives, to connect more fully with those around us, to help us love ourselves, and even to help improve our sexual prowess.

- Certain crystals are said to have properties that improve our psychic powers. We can meditate with them to increase these powers and help us to open up our third eye.

- While some of the benefits of crystals are more ethereal than others, there are those based strongly in science, such as the way that rose quartz, and smoky quartz have been used to improve the health of our skin by being included in beauty products.

- Just because you have a personal relationship with your crystal doesn't mean that your crystal can't also help your plants. Adding the right crystal to the soil around your plants can help to keep them strong and healthy.

- Crystals make up an important part of feng shui, and crystal decorations play a big role in opening up the energy of a room in order to create a much happier and healthier environment that promotes positivity.

- Certain crystals are literally healing crystals in the sense that they can help us to reduce our pain and find relief from the pressures that weigh us down physically, mentally, and spiritually.

- One of the most common uses for healing crystals is to help us to increase the amount of happiness we have in our lives. Some crystals are used to directly enhance our overall sense of joy, while others are used to reduce the amount of depression and anxiety that we experience.

- Practices such as meditation or contemplation with or on our crystals can be a great way to find an island of calm inside that helps us to not overreact to situations, but rather to take events as they come with careful consideration.

- There are also crystals that are used to help remove or prevent negativity energies from overtaking our lives. These crystals are protective and can help us to ward off evil influences that want to ruin our daily lived experience.

In the next chapter, you will learn all about the crystals that help heal our emotions. If you suffer from depression or anxiety, then you can find great relief through the use of the right healing crystals. There are crystals that help to keep us motivated and others that can bring wealth into our lives. There are crystals that help us to experience and find love and others that promote happiness and reduce stress. Regardless of the emotion, there is a healing crystal that will help.

# CHAPTER TWO

# BEST CRYSTALS TO HEAL YOUR EMOTIONS

Far beyond just our physical health, healing crystals are effective at helping us to heal our emotions, invite positive emotions, and to actualize an abundant lifestyle that encourages us to chase our goals and aim high. If we want to live a life that is as meaningful as possible, as positive as can be, and filled with happiness, love, health, and serenity, then we should seek out the help of crystals. They'll make these goals much easier to achieve.

With that said, the biggest question becomes, "What crystal should I use?" This is another question that isn't easy to answer. The answer is going to be based on what you want your healing crystals to help you with. If you are seeking motivation, then you'll use different stones than you would if you're after love. Anxiety would use different stones, as well. Of course, each of these categories will have a little crossover, but no category will be composed of the same crystals as another. One of the reasons for this is the huge variety of crystals. Happy Glastonbury's list of crystals mentions that there are almost 200 of them, while their A to Z list of crystals has 255 different examples, including the various permutations of each crystal. For an example of this, consider that the site lists apricot, black, blue-banded, blue lace, crazy lace, green, moss, purple, tree, and yellow agates. They're all agates, but a yellow agate is going to have a different energy compared to a purple one.

To get a better sense of the many kinds of crystals, this chapter divides up our emotional and lived spheres so we can look at which crystals are used in matters of love, depression, wealth, or motivation. If you already know the areas that you need an assist, then this can help you to pinpoint which crystals you should begin using. If you aren't yet sure as to what you want healing crystals to help you out with, then this chapter might enable you to get ideas, but you are going to find more useful information in chapter three and our discussion aimed at introducing beginners to their first crystals.

**Crystals for Depression and Anxiety**

If you have ever suffered from anxiety or depression, then you know exactly how many such issues can ruin your life. They can make it impossible to get out of bed. They can make you nervous about even leaving the house or picking up the phone. These are debilitating conditions that can feel like a noose wrapped around your neck. When you are facing them, you may feel there is no way to get help. If you are dealing with depression and anxiety, you should seek out educated and certified assistance. However, therapy and other solutions of this ilk aren't performed in a vacuum. You still need to live and go about your life in between your sessions. These periods can feel like drowning in the ocean while waiting for another island to set your feet on (your next therapy session).

Crystals might not be enough to get you out of the ocean of depression, but they can act as a raft, which helps you to navigate the rough waters. They become tools that work alongside the therapy so as to provide you with relief. As you grow stronger and get a better understanding of your depression or anxiety, you may find that you need fewer therapy sessions. Despite this, I am convinced you will find yourself holding onto your crystals as they will continue to help you so long as you let them. So, without further ado, let's take a look at which crystals are the most effective for tackling these dark beasts.

First up is citrine. In specific, you should look for citrine that is closer to being transparent rather than yellow like quartz. A clear citrine of this type will work a lot more effectively for the purposes of helping to alleviate depression. When used for dealing with depression, citrine doesn't add value to your life the same way that crystals for happiness do. Instead, it helps to remove the negative energies surrounding you and causing your depression. If you can find a rarer smoky citrine, then this is even more effective. Smoky citrine is a naturally forming citrine that looks almost like it has cigarette smoke trapped inside, and it can be easy to tell the difference between the two when compared together. This smoky citrine provides the added benefit of helping to lift your mood, while also working to remove the negativity that has infected you.

Another great healing crystal is sunstone. This beautiful looking gem is made up of a mixture of yellowish-orange and pink that immediately makes you think of happier days. There are lots of little sparkles in the stone which allows it to positively glow when the light hits it. This is fitting since sunstone will help to leave you glowing. The light color reflects the way that sunstone helps to lift your mood to invite a more positive, bright energy into your life. As you begin to work with healing crystals, you will likely discover that some are quite heavy. Not in a physical sense, but their energies are too intense for some beginners. Sunstone has a gentle energy that helps to heal, but it doesn't overpower. That makes it a wonderful choice for those dealing with depression and for those who aren't yet experienced in managing the energies of these crystals.

We talked about smoky citrine, but it isn't the only smoky crystal to make the list. In fact, citrine is a kind of quartz, and another great crystal for helping with depression is smoky quartz. This quartz has a very dark color, almost as if the smoke trapped inside had stained the surface. That might sound unappealing, but it is actually quite a beautiful kind of quartz, very different from how we normally think of it. Smoky quartz works similarly to citrine in that it helps to remove the negative energy from your life. The less negative energy around you, the less negativity weighing down your mind and perverting your thoughts. This is a very powerful crystal, though it has a power that isn't overly intrusive. However, you need to make sure that you cleanse smoky quartz on a regular basis. If it is left to absorb the negative without ever being cleansed, then you will find that it starts to invite more negativity into your life. As long as you purify it on a regular basis, it will continue to help improve your mind and energy. You can find out how to cleanse your healing crystals in chapter five.

Another terrific choice is rose quartz. You might begin to notice a pattern here. Generally speaking, quartz crystals are among the most powerful for dealing with depression and negative mental energies. As this is the case, rose quartz fits in perfectly with citrine and smoky quartz. This type of quartz has a very light pink color that almost borders on white. Instead of removing negative energies, this type of quartz invites in lots of warmth and positive energies, which can help to bring comfort to those facing the turbulent experience that is depression. Rose quartz is also used for helping to reduce stress, and it also promotes a level of self-love that might seem absent when we are depressed. For the most benefit from this powerful crystal, keep it close to your heart in a necklace or even simply by storing it in your breast pocket.

Angel Aura is a type of quartz that has been treated with platinum or silver. This produces a lovely shine. It has an iridescent quality, which is only enhanced by the light, almost pastel colors, that the crystal takes on. This particular quartz crystal can be too powerful for beginners, but those that have the experience to benefit from it can immediately feel the way that it begins to work. Hold it in your hand to feel how it sends vibrations up your arm and deep into your soul. This makes it an effective tool for dealing with a negative mindset. Simply take the angel aura in your hand, close your eyes and focus on it for a few moments. Right away, you will feel how hope starts to return to you. It helps to open up your heart and let you invite in the positive healing energies that are all around us every day.

You might have noticed the way crystals of specific colors help in dealing with negative experiences. Smoky crystals are extremely useful in pulling out negative energy and trapping it, thereby removing it from you, and keeping it in the crystal until you are able to cleanse it. Also common is the way that lighter colored crystals help to bring positive energy into your life. Carnelian is a crystal that is mostly red, but lighter points of white make some parts of it closer to orange or pink. Carnelian is a great crystal for lifting your mood, bringing in positive energy, and reducing the levels of anxiety in your life. It can also help to keep you motivated, making it a versatile healing crystal that could easily fit in several of the categories that we're exploring this chapter.

**Crystals for Stress and Anxiety**

Stress and anxiety are no laughing matter. They may not be considered to be quite as bad as clinical depression, but that doesn't mean they can't also deeply impact your life and reduce your level of comfort. If you are dealing with anxiety, then you may want to consider talking to a medical professional about what help is available to you. If you are dealing with high levels of anxiety, then you will want to adopt practices such as meditation or gratitude journaling, both of which are proven to help reduce the levels of cortisol that flow through your body on a daily basis. All of these are positive actions you can take to help the effects of these problems, but they don't need to be the only steps you take. There are lots of healing crystals that will help you in managing these feelings, and you can even combine them into your healthy practices, such as including one of the following crystals into your meditation routine. When it comes to anxiety, stress, and even depression, it is important to use every resource available to you as these issues should never be taken lightly.

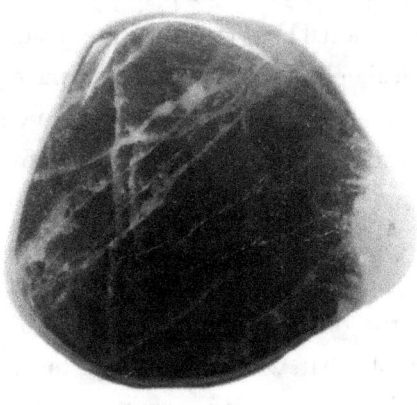

If you're looking to reduce anxiety and stress in your life, perhaps there is no better choice than sodalite. This beautiful blue crystal has been given the nickname, "the stone of peace," and if you have ever dealt with stress, then you know how vital it is to find some peace of mind in the midst of your struggles. This crystal is used to help you achieve this and to reduce the likelihood of panic attacks. This crystal is powerful enough to work even when it is only kept in your pocket, though, ideally, you will want to hold in your hand to let it suffuse through your body. Its blue color is associated with peace, calm, and relaxation. It helps to reduce the overall level of stress you are feeling. Sodalite is also useful in bringing confidence into your life and helping you to express yourself more fully, which makes it a great choice for anyone preparing to give a public speech. Reducing the stress and helping you express yourself is a powerful combination for tackling anxiety and spotlight jitters.

Turning to another blue crystal, we have kyanite. One of the things that can cause a lot of stress and anxiety in your life is when your spiritual nature isn't properly integrated into your life. Losing sight of your spiritual nature can cause you to feel disconnected from the world around you, and it can make you anxious without even knowing it or realizing why. One of the ways we can find our spiritual selves again is through meditation or mindfulness retreats, but these aren't always an option. A quicker and easier way to reach that spiritual self is to practice short meditation sessions using kyanite. This blue crystal is fantastic in helping to connect you to that spiritual level and to realign the chakras in your body to keep them open and flowing fully. If you are dealing with anxiety, stress, fear, anger, or more of those negative feelings, kyanite can help you to release them rather than allow them to stick and fester in your mind. The coolest part of kyanite is the fact that it doesn't absorb these negative emotions the way that a crystal like smoky quartz does. This means that you don't ever need to cleanse kyanite, making it one of the most effective and easy ways to get help dealing with your stress and anxiety.

Moving away from the lighter colored crystals, we find shungite. This dark stone is such a deep blue color that it often appears to be pure black. Shungite is recommended for the way that it helps to protect wearers from electrical-magnetic fields such as those produced by today's plethora of electronics. If you have a lot of stress coming from your workplace, then adding some shungite to your desk will help to bring it down. It is also great for the way it helps to protect you from negative energies that would otherwise bring you down and weigh heavily on your mind. Shungite does need to be purified frequently; otherwise, it will grow less effective until it finally fails to provide any value at all. But if you make it a habit to cleanse it, shungite can be one of the most important crystals in your collection.

In complete contrast of color is Himalayan salt rock. Mostly white, though sometimes pink, Himalayan salt rock is used to help remove negative energy from the body so that you can stay positive and let go of the stress and anxiety that weighs you down. You can find Himalayan salt in the grocery store, though this isn't quite the same. You want to purchase it in rock form rather than ground up. This rock form of the salt is used in salt lamps that create a rainstorm-like effect through electromagnetics. If you purchase Himalayan salt rock for your diet, then it will have some positive influence, but as a healing crystal, you should have some in a vial that you can keep on your person or attached to a necklace. If you have more than you need for this, you can add a little to a bath. Himalayan salt rock is high in vibrations and can turn any bath into a cleansing experience that helps you to literally wash away the worry and anxiety that you're dealing with. When used regularly, this can help you to correct your sleeping schedule and keep you feeling connected to the world around you and your life. These are aspects of existence that we often lose sight of when we are prey to fears and anxiety.

We spoke about rose quartz in the previous section, but it is worth briefly mentioning it again here. Not only is it excellent for helping you to overcome depression, but it can be as effective in tackling anxiety and reducing stress. If it is stress that you are trying to deal with, then rose quartz should be kept in a location where you can readily see it, as it will help to serve as a visual reminder to take care of yourself and relax. For added benefits, put a little Himalayan salt rock into a bath and keep some rose quartz on the side of the tub. These will help to calm you down and remind you to really take part in the bath, to be in the moment with it, and to see it as an opportunity to relax, time that is meant for you.

In the last section, we looked at sunstone, but this time around, we're looking at the reverse: moonstone. This beautiful, milky white stone looks so appealing that you could almost eat it right up. Moonstone has strong ties to motherhood, and it is recommended to keep it on you if you wish to increase your chances of getting pregnant, as well as to keep the pregnancy healthy and to help reduce the pain and discomfort of childbirth. This makes the moonstone far more effective for women than for men. Part of this is the strong connection it has to female hormones, and it can help women to let go of stress and realign their natural intuition with the world around them. If you are feeling lost or worried, hold a piece of moonstone in your hand while you meditate and focus your attention on the healing vibrations that it emits.

Note, men can still use moonstone, of course, but it won't have the same profound connection that it has with women.

The final crystal that we'll look at for stress and anxiety is howlite. While it also happens to be white, it doesn't look much like moonstone at all. Instead, the white of howlite is very bold and dense, and it often has veins of grey or black lines that snake through it to give it a really neat appearance. In fact, one of the best ways of using howlite is to meditate with it while tracing these dark links with a finger. When we are overly worried, we often aren't getting enough sleep, and this only serves to make the issue worse. Place a piece of howlite underneath your pillow to benefit from its soothing energies so that you can get to sleep much easier. Howlite is such a calming crystal that it is often recommended to help teach patience. It is also a crystal that promotes understanding and wisdom, which helps to reduce the struggles you experience in life by removing feelings of anxiety or anger, emotions that can make you lose sight of your spiritual self. While it is most commonly placed under the pillow, you can also keep some in a pocket or add a piece to a bracelet so as to carry the benefits with you throughout the day.

## Crystals for Happiness

If you are dealing with depression or anxiety, then it is readily clear how important it is to get help in minimizing the damage of these negative emotions. But we can also approach it from the other side. It might be less apparent that we can make our lives better by increasing the positivity and happiness that we are feeling. We shouldn't only be using crystals in order to remove the bad. They are also amazing tools that let us amplify the positive. It is great to be happy, but it is even better to be ecstatic. You'll notice a couple of the crystals that we look at in this section have been mentioned previously. This is important to note because it helps us to see the way that these crystals don't just work to achieve one result. They can actually help us to achieve several goals at once, such as increasing contentment while also reducing stress. Of course, reducing stress will help us to reach our happiness more readily, and so these goals aren't mutually exclusive in any sense of the word. They're just different paths to the same destination.

Let's start by looking at those crystals which we have already seen. You will remember that quartz is strongly linked to helping remove negativity. Rose quartz is often used for love, but it also helps us to reach into the compassion inside of us. When we can tap into our compassion, we get better at applying it to ourselves, and this lets us practice self-love. Not only does self-love help us to reduce our depression, but it helps us to be more content and happy with who we are and the life that we are living.

Smoky quartz is another that we've seen in regards to depression. This one helps to take negativity out of our lives, but it requires us to cleanse it often so that it keeps working. Along with this, smoky quartz is also good for helping bring a more positive energy into our lives. Part of this is the fact that the negative is removed, but removing the negative doesn't necessarily bring in the positive. Thankfully, smoky quartz also invites rays of positivity to fill up the space where our negativity once was.

Clear quartz also removes negative energy and makes room for positivity. Clear quartz has been called the master healer because it helps not only to remove negativity, but also helps purify body, mind, and soul. This is necessary to open up our chakras and prevent unconscious blockages which prevent us from living our lives with as much joyfulness as possible. We discussed the way that losing sight of our spiritual selves can bring a lot of darkness into our lives and make us feel lost. Clear quartz is one of the most effective crystals we have to enable us to reconnect with our spiritual selves.

Finally, the last of the crystals we have already explored in this chapter is citrine. This crystal has a very free and open energy, which invites us to feel confident and content, a great combination for bringing more happiness to our souls. As with any of these crystals we've seen before, citrine can be used specifically to promote more positivity. What that means is you don't need to reach for these crystals only when there is negativity to be removed. With that understood, let's move on to some new crystals.

Amazonite has a lot in common with citrine in the way that both crystals help to create a more hopeful experience with a free loving attitude. When we try to stop up our love and add barriers to it, we do a great disservice to our happiness. Amazonite helps us to stay authentic, with a heart open up to the world as a whole. This is fantastic because, most of the time, we aren't even aware of the way we have created barriers around our hearts. Amazonite helps to break these down and let us tap into the limitless happiness that is inside of each and every one of us.

Amethyst is another gorgeous crystal, as many of them are. While amethyst helps us to be more positive and happy, it also helps us to stay calm. When we face trouble by panicking or freaking out, we only serve to make our anxiety stronger. But when we face struggles with calmness, we are able to stay closer to our happiness. Struggles no longer take that happiness away from us. We can find the time to look directly at our struggles and see them for what they are. When we do this, we are more readily able to tackle and deal with them without losing our positivity in the process. Keep a piece of amethyst close to your heart to help stay calm and open. That will help us to stay more tightly connected to our spiritual selves, which is always a positive for our soul.

If you are looking for crystals to help with happiness, but you aren't entirely sure which to go with, it is a good bet to stick to the color yellow. These crystals bring to mind the sun and the way the brightness of its rays dispel the darkness of the night. Tiger's eye and yellow jasper are two examples of yellow crystals that serve to prove this point explicitly. Tiger's eye is fantastic for helping us tap into our inner strength and not let our happiness be diminished. Keep a piece of tiger's eye close at hand for any time you need to tap into this strength. It is also useful in helping us to expand our consciousness to see from different perspectives. That makes it excellent for anyone who works in a creative field or one in which they need to generate unique ideas. Yellow jasper, on the other hand, is almost entirely focused on bringing a positive light into our lives. It can help to bring confidence, though we are always more confident when we are happy, and so this could be seen as a reflection of the way it opens us up to the nourishing nature of reality.

Black tourmaline seems to go against everything mentioned in the last paragraph, but this isn't technically true. We might naturally assume that if yellow, light-colored stones bring positivity, then darker stones would bring more downbeat qualities. But black tourmaline is used to remove fear from our lives and to help us keep our heads rather than panic. If you are facing a difficult time, then this crystal should be one of the first that you turn to for assistance. It has the added benefit of helping to bring more physical energy, which is so important when going through a hard situation. Negativity often leaves us feeling weak and exhausted, so black tourmaline works to counter this. To get the most significant benefit to your happiness, combine black tourmaline with one of the other crystals on this list.

The final one we'll look at for happiness is ametrine. This crystal also has a lot in common with citrine, which you might notice from their spelling alone. But, more than the spelling, they share a focus on helping us to stay connected to our spiritual selves while pushing negativity away from us. Ametrine is a gender-neutral crystal that allows us to tap into our male and female energies. We are all composed of energies of both kinds, with men having more male energy and women having more female energy. But, as men or women, we need to be in tune with both of these energies to have a healthy and fulfilling experience throughout life. Ametrine helps us to get in touch with these energies in a positive manner, not favoring one over the other. Hold onto ametrine when you meditate or consider placing it over your heart while lying down.

**Crystals for Love**

One of the most profound elements that unite human beings is the way that we all want to feel loved. We have a biological urge to find a partner and raise a family, to keep our name going. Even those of us who don't want children still want love. To find a partner that respects you and helps to keep you productive, happy, and healthy has motivated millions of people and thousands upon thousands of stories across film, plays, and television. Yet these days there is a tendency to feel a deep loneliness which seems particular to our 21st-century living. We have websites to help us meet partners, and yet we still find ourselves alone. It can feel like there is no way to get over this, like love doesn't belong in our lives.

This is just ridiculous. Of course, we deserve love. We'll find it, too, so long as we look for it. But that doesn't mean that we can't take some steps to help *it* find *us*. One of the ways we do this is by turning to healing crystals with the properties of love. These can help to remind us that we deserve to be loved. This is great because it gives us a better aura, one that invites love to us. What's more, the right crystal can help to attract that love as strongly as any dating site ever could. We've encountered a couple of these stones, but there are far more left to discover. So if you are looking for some assistance in finding romance, then you should be reaching for one of these amazing crystals.

We've covered rose quartz a couple of times, but it is fantastic for increasing the amount of love in your life, specifically the love that you feel inside your heart. We also discussed moonstone, though not in the context of love. Moonstone has a long tradition as a wedding gift, as it is supposed to bring good luck in love. It is important to gift moonstone to both the bride and the groom, as this goes into older European traditions. It is said that if two people wear moonstone on the night of a full moon, then they will fall in love when the light of the moon reflects off the crystal. Traditions like this exist as one of the ways our ancestors made sense of the healing powers of crystals such as these.

Amber is such a beautiful and vibrant crystal that we named it for its color. You'll note that the orange color ties it closely to tiger's eye and yellow jasper. Like those two crystals, amber can attract a lot of positivity into your life, but it is used more often for love rather than happiness. If you are looking to use amber for its romantic properties, then you will benefit most from wearing it close to your heart, as opening up this chakra will do wonders for your love life. This crystal not only attracts romance and love, but it helps to attract your desires in general, be they happiness, health, wealth, love, or peace. It is also said that amber has protective qualities that help to keep you free from evil influences.

When it comes to love, the color most strongly associated is red. The brighter and bolder the red, the more profoundly this connection pops out. Think about lipstick and hearts, how desire and sexuality are intimately connected to red. Garnet is one of the most stunningly bright red crystals and one that absorbs and pulls in intensely romantic and erotic energies. If you are looking to find love, then wearing garnet is a must. Plus, we know that wearing bold colors like garnet help to make us feel more confident, which in turn further helps us to attract a mate. Garnet is also used in helping to enhance the sexual connection between lovers. To get the most benefits, put a garnet next to the bed or have your partner hold it in their hand as you initiate a lovemaking session.

More pink than red, rhodochrosite is also closely connected to the heart. As it happens, rhodochrosite has been given the expressive title, "The Stone of the Compassionate Heart." With a title like that, it can be no surprise that this gorgeous crystal is amazing for helping your tap into the love all around you. Not only does this help to attract romantic love, but it is also used quite often to help with emotional healing. If you have experienced a painful breakup, rhodochrosite will help you to get over the heightened emotions that come with the territory while also helping you to attract a more fitting and compatible romantic partner. Plus, like garnet, this crystal has been connected to improved sexual relations with your partner. Where garnet is more closely connected to the erotic, rhodochrosite is involved more with intimacy as a whole.

Rose tourmaline has an almost blood-red appearance. This has led to rose tourmaline being connected to vampires in popular culture, but in reality, this red should be thought of in a less sensational, but profound light, as closer to the lifeblood that pumps through your heart. It is this blood that keeps you alive, but it is also this same blood that passes through your heart, and with it comes all of the love that you have ever felt. Rose tourmaline taps into this well of love inside us and helps to open up both the chakras in the heart and those in the head. This helps us to connect our love to our spiritual selves and to feel a connection far deeper than the purely physical. Rose tourmaline helps us to link these two elements of ourselves to create a flow of energy more in tune with the natural ebb and flow of romantic passion.

Yet another wonderful crystal for matters of the heart is red agate, and again, we see just how powerfully linked the color red is to our love and compassion. Everyone would agree that the best marriages are those that bring a sense of stability and security to the lovers while leaving enough room for them to grow and experience the many gifts that life offers. Red agate helps to strengthen all of these, and it should be worn by both lovers rather than just one of them. This stone helps us to open up the root chakra, which is the chakra that allows us to feel at home in our body and connected to the world around us. With this connection comes a more profound sense of being linked to our partners, and the fears of jealousy have a tendency to fade away once lovers begin wearing red agate together. If you aren't in a relationship yet, red agate can help you to feel balanced, but it isn't particularly useful in drawing a romantic partner to you the same way as some of the others we've looked at.

Lapis Lazuli breaks from our pattern of red crystals. This blue crystal is used primarily for calming the soul and keeping us steady and grounded in the face of hardship. But this turns out to be especially useful in matters of the heart as well. We often struggle with jealousy, for example. When we get jealous, we want to fly off the handle and accuse our partner of being dishonest or unfaithful. But the calming aura of lapis lazuli can help us to keep our calm and look at the situation with open eyes. When you do this, you are able to more clearly see the relationship you have with your partner for what it is, and you can see the way that misunderstandings occur. For this reason, it is useful to keep lapis lazuli on you at all times. This powerful crystal is also used to help fix the bridges between you and those around you, bridges that you may have thought you had burned. Furthermore, this amazing crystal helps us to get more in touch with ourselves so that we can understand the ways we unintentionally hurt those around us. What this is useful for is gaining the knowledge necessary to better ourselves and apologize. So powerful is this crystal when it comes to interpersonal relationships, that there is even folklore that posits that giving lapis lazuli as a gift is to make a friendship that will last until the end of time.

Even if it isn't an endless relationship, gifting lapis lazuli to your lover can be a way of deeply bonding.

Our final crystal for matters of love is the opal. This multifaceted crystal is used to draw love towards us, while also helping us to more deeply understand our passions and desires. Keep an opal close at hand, and use it in meditation to help open your heart to the world, and to purge the negativity from your system. By helping you to let go of the unconscious stoppages which prevent you from loving fully, opal can assist you in having a more honest and clear dialogue with your partner (or potential partner). Openness and honesty tend to reward us in spades with love, happiness, and wealth, and so an opal should absolutely be a part of your romantic toolkit if you turn to healing crystals for support with the love you foster in your life.

**Crystals for Wealth**

Less an emotion and more a desire, wealth is one of the primary motivating factors of human existence. We think of wealth primarily in regard to money and income. This isn't wrong, as these are one definition of wealth. But we should also remember that wealth can be intangible, too. We experience a sense of wealth when we look around and see that we have fostered many meaningful relationships. We feel our wealth when we realize that we have built up a successful career and have gained the respect of our peers. When we speak of an abundance of wealth, money is only one way that manifests itself.

This section will primarily focus on money, but these kinds of wealth are closely related. One of the biggest ways in which we cut ourselves off from wealth is psychological. We convince ourselves that we aren't deserving of it and that it will never come to us. Working with crystals can help us to get over this so that not only do we draw wealth towards us, but we are also able to act on it when it comes into our presence. This combination of attraction, then action, is one of the most powerful and meaningful ways of using crystals that we have. Again, we'll start with a couple of crystals that are familiar to us by this point.

We've seen citrine used for several purposes before, but what we haven't mentioned is its nickname: The Lucky Merchant's Stone. We spoke primarily about natural citrine, and this is actually quite rare. When it comes to dealing with depression, natural citrine is the way to go. But most citrine is created by taking amethyst and using heat to treat it. While you wouldn't want to use this form of citrine for your depression, you can certainly use it for the purposes of attracting wealth. With a title like The Lucky Merchant's Stone, citrine has strong links to financial success. If you are planning a business endeavor, you will want to keep citrine close at hand. One way in which to use crystals for wealth is to create a section of your house, room, or office in which you store and set out your intentions for success and money. Citrine is a great addition to one of these displays as it doesn't just invite wealth to us, but it also reminds us that our wealth is exponentially more valuable when we share it with those around us.

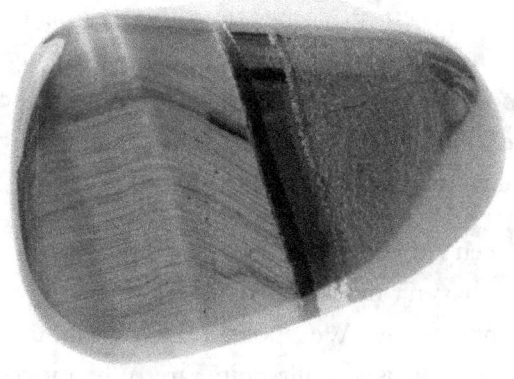

Tiger's eye is another healing crystal that we looked at. Called the stone of the mind, tiger's eye is used to help us to manifest our dreams to bring about a change in our lives. This is not necessarily tied to wealth, as the change we want could be to find love, health, or happiness. But often the change we want most is to find success in our field and to earn enough money to live comfortably. When our dreams are connected to a sense of wealth, that is the time to use tiger's eye to invite reality to meet us halfway. This is important to note, as we can't expect our healing crystals to do all the work. They help us to achieve our goals, but if we never get off the couch to even try to achieve them ourselves, then they will never happen. But so long as you are willing to do the work, tiger's eye will help you to succeed in your actions. If you are starting a new business, protect your wealth, or invite positivity and good fortune into your life, then you should use a piece of tiger's eye. It can be kept on you to help you to prevent wasteful spending when you are out and about, or it can be added to your wealth display to interact with and assist the crystals you are already using.

Quartz is also used to help attract wealth. Specifically, clear quartz crystals. However, to attract wealth, you should only use clear quartz in combination with another crystal. That's because clear quartz can amplify the energy from the crystals around it. So if clear quartz is the only crystal in your wealth display, you aren't going to get any benefits regarding your wealth. It needs something to work on, and there is just nothing for it to help amplify. You will get benefits from it, keep in mind, just not in regard to wealth. Clear quartz is called The Master Healer, and you will get benefits in that regard. But, if you add clear quartz to a wealth display that already has a crystal or two related to attracting wealth, then you will amplify their energies, and make the whole display that much more effective. It should be noted that you can technically infuse clear quartz with any intention, which means that you could use it to attract wealth on its own with enough work and effort on your part, but it is far, far easier to use it for its amplification properties. It is like trying to swim against a river. Technically, you can do it, but it is far more effective if you go with the flow of the river instead.

Next up is fool's gold, otherwise known as pyrite. This stone is amazingly attractive to look at, as it mixes elements of rock with gold to create a glittering appearance that mesmerizes. Any healing crystal of this sort that captures the light to sparkle is a terrific choice for a meditation crystal, as its very appearance helps us to enter into a contemplative state. Hold a piece of pyrite in your hand and focus on it. You can keep it still or move it around in the palm of your hand; either way works. The name fool's gold implies a negative, as nobody wants to be considered a fool. But this name comes to us from the history of trading. People would try to pass off fool's gold as plain old gold. Anyone who fell for this trade was being duped, and was, thus, the fool. But we aren't reaching for pyrite because we think it's gold. We use it because it has a strong force that attracts money. Rather than giving away your fool's gold, keep it close at hand whenever you enter into business situations. It doesn't matter if you are setting up a new business, depositing a cheque, or making an investment, keeping this close at hand invites the universe to look kindly on our transaction so that it will be profitable. We can also use pyrite to help us tap into our courage, as its name comes from the Greek word for fire, and it helps to remind us of the infinite fire of passion that we have inside at any given moment.

One of the key elements we need in order to be successful is luck. It is disappointing to hear that, no matter how well conceived our plans are, no matter how many factors we calculate for, we still need a dose of luck if our plans are to be successful. You might write up a business plan that seems absolutely solid and sound, but then the world can shut down because of an illness. There is too much randomness for us to not rely, to some measure, on luck. But we can improve our luck by using a lucky charm such as a piece of free jade. These crystals have healing properties that can help us to open ourselves up and stop repeating the same mistakes, but they are also fantastic for inviting luck. There is an ancient tradition in China which sees jade as one of the most important substances known to mankind. It was to invoke luck and good fortune that they made jade statues and gave jade as gifts to each other. But the connection of jade and luck goes far beyond Asia and can be seen in cultures as far apart as Russia and Mexico. Jade is especially powerful when used in meditation. It helps us to focus our energy to keep us moving towards our goals. By inviting luck and keeping us going forward, jade brings us much good fortune. Beyond meditation, wearing a jade necklace can let us carry this luck with us throughout our daily lives.

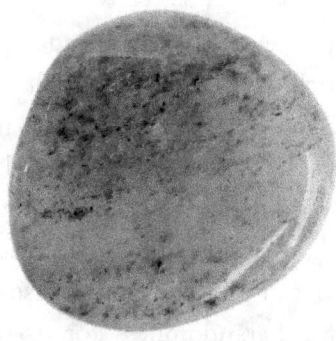

Another gorgeous green stone we can use for attracting wealth is green aventurine. This smooth stone is called the Stone of Opportunity, and if that name doesn't hint at its relationship with attracting wealth, then nothing will. Green aventurine has an intriguing energy that is used to help us regain wealth that we lost due to poorly thought-out plans. Bad investments, wasteful spending, and poor impulse control can all leave us with much less wealth than we are supposed to have. These losses can be devastating and lead us down a path of regret. But what we have lost can come back to us, and green aventurine is foundational in making sure that happens. Green aventurine should be worn in a necklace that hangs over your heart chakra. You may want to wear this throughout the day, but you definitely must wear it while meditating. Some crystals are better served by being held onto during meditation. Green aventurine works best the closer it is to your heart chakra so that its vibrations can help to open it back up and invite abundance into your being.

Love has strong connections to the color red, and happiness is often supported by yellow crystals. You might have figured out already that the color green has a clear link to wealth. Many people seem to think this is due to the fact that paper currency is green, but this only takes into account an American's currency. Yet we see the connection between wealth and the color green in many different cultures. It is more likely that the USA's currency was chosen to be green due to this symbolism and not the other way around. Green aventurine and jade are powerful crystals for attracting wealth, and they are further joined by peridot. Sometimes called the Study Stone, this crystal looks like a green ruby, and the way light passes through it creates an entrancing effect. Peridot is used similarly to clear quartz, in that it can help to boost the energies of the crystals it is used around. More than money itself, peridot is connected to our desires. If you desire love, peridot can help to boost the love-attracting nature of other crystals. If you desire money, then it definitely provides a boost. Add peridot to your wealth display or use it in a crystal grid to get the most benefits. To deeply connect it to wealth, consider creating a grid that uses only green crystals as this level of uniformity can help to make your intentions clearer.

Another green stone we use is the Stone of Hope, Success, and Abundance, otherwise known as amazonite. This stone is very rough, with a turquoise color that is interwoven with webs of white. When you look at it, amazonite seems almost like a piece of the ocean had been captured in a solid form. Not directly tied to money itself, amazonite is used to attract abundance. That might refer to money, but also love, respect, and power could fit into the description. If you are in a position of financial leadership, then amazonite can be a great ally in helping you to stay cool and focused so that you can tackle any issue that arises. Since wealth flows naturally from a successful business, strong leadership is an important and attractive feature to improve through the use of a healing crystal.

Let's close out this section on perhaps the greenest crystal of all. Malachite is sometimes called the Stone of Transformation, and this is seen in the way that the colors shift from light green to dark green and all the shades in between. While jade is a dark green, malachite is a mixture of dark and light green, which makes each shade stand out more clearly through contrast. Malachite is used in removing negativity, making it a healing crystal that you may want to include in grids meant for tackling depression. But the most significant feature of malachite is the way that it attracts energy to it. Not just wealth, but energy itself. This can be the energy or abundance or positive energy that brings happiness and calm. Another name for malachite was the Stone for Merchants, which more readily links it to wealth. For the best results using malachite, you may choose to keep it in a grid or a display, but it offers the most support when it is kept in your purse or wallet. Our wallets are most readily associated with wealth, and so by having a piece of malachite there, we invite abundance in that specific direction and form.

**Crystals for Courage and Motivation**

We could all use a little more courage in our lives. Sometimes our bravery is blocked due to depression or anxiety, but often we don't have the ability to access our courage even when we are feeling happy and successful. This is extremely frustrating because each one of us has courage inside. This reservoir is connected to our motivation in a symbiotic relationship. When we have motivation, we need our courage to act on it, and when we can tap into our courage, it becomes easier to keep ourselves motivated. But motivation and bravery often don't come to us as effortlessly as we might like. Sometimes we need assistance. This can come in the form of a spiritual practice like meditation or classes from a life coach or mentor. But these are just some of the more popular ways to access these qualities. One that is simple and surprisingly effective is, you guessed it, healing crystals.

One of the powerful attributes of healing crystals is the way they give back what you put in. For example, when you turn to a crystal for help in your love life, you get back energy that helps you to attract love and abundance into your life. Choosing crystals with strong ties to the heart helps to increase this return, but you can get benefits even when using the wrong ones. Again, the metaphor of swimming against the current works perfectly here. If we want to get the most benefit to our courage, we should select crystals that help to keep us motivated and feeling brave. However, it is important to consider what you want the courage for. If it is to find financial success, then you should first turn to crystals that invite wealth. If it is for love, then turn to the crystals we looked at in that section. Use the crystals for courage to help amplify and supplement those that are specific to your goals. This will help you to get the most direct benefits for what you desire. It is like seeing a specialist instead of a general practitioner; the results will be much more specific to your needs.

Carnelian is a great choice for motivation, especially if you are looking for motivation to start a new business venture or to keep pushing through a hard time. We often come up against challenges in our lives, and when this happens, it can be easy to retreat and shrink away. To face a challenge is to face a hardship, something that pushes us to grow and be more than we were. We all have this capacity for growth, but we often convince ourselves that we don't. We like to tell ourselves that we are less than we are, and this is a terribly poisonous attitude that can greatly damage our chances of success. If you are having a hard time staying motivated and tapping into your courage, carnelian should be a go-to crystal for you. This crystal helps us to open up our sacral chakra and tap into the unlimited creativity inside of us. It enables us to come up with unique solutions to the challenges we face. One of the biggest things that takes motivation away from us is when we convince ourselves that there is only one answer to a problem and that it isn't a good one. Carnelian helps us to see that there are many solutions to every problem, and with a little bit of consideration and courage, we can discover the way that is right for us.

Despite its bright red color, ruby isn't associated with love like many of the red crystals. Instead, this beautiful stone is associated with nobility and a sense of pride. Its strong vibrational energy helps us to stay rejuvenated so that we can stick it out through even the hardest challenges. This energy can be fantastic for more than just facing obstacles, though. Consider meditating with ruby in the morning so that you can meet each day with more natural energy than normal. One of the factors that drain away our motivation and courage is a lack of energy, and so this helps to cut out the fatigue and keep us meeting each day with robust confidence and a sense of opportunity.

Blue apatite is linked to inspiration. Inspiration itself is tightly linked to motivation. If you've ever had a burst of inspiration, then you know the motivating energy that follows. When inspiration hits, it suddenly feels like nothing else matters, that the only important thing in the world is to act on the inspiration. We might not even consider this feeling to be a sense of motivation because it is so tightly linked to the inspiration. But inspiration provokes motivation, as inspiration itself is not an action or a replicable experience. We can be hit by inspiration when looking at a painting or a cloud, but then the next painting or next cloud won't trigger a thing in our souls. We need inspiration to push us to motivation, but then we need that motivation to carry us through to our next actions. As inspiration fades, it requires more courage to keep going. This holy trinity can benefit from the use of blue apatite to increase the likelihood that inspiration will strike, while also helping us to stay concentrated on our goals. Focus itself is an element of motivation, as we want to push ourselves harder and further when we are focused, and thus we are actually using motivation without realizing it. Blue apatite is such a powerful crystal because of the way it helps us tap into this motivation in a subtle but profound way.

We saw that yellow jasper could help us to tap into a deeper sense of happiness and bring positivity to our lives. That's far from the only purpose that jasper serves, though it is the primary purpose of yellow jasper. If we are looking for help staying motivated and confident, we may want to use yellow jasper, but red jasper is more potent for achieving our purpose. This bright crystal is powerful yet gentle, with an aura that doesn't demand much from the person wearing it. In especially stressful times, we can find ourselves losing our motivation. While you should turn to a healing crystal with stress relief properties, these won't necessarily bring back your motivation. Consider your body as a house for your energy. When you are motivated, your motivation is renting the house. But then comes stress to evict your motivation and take over. You might evict stress by using a healing crystal for stress relief, but this doesn't immediately bring motivation back as a tenant. You need to extend an invitation and coax it back in, and red jasper is one of the most effective tools for achieving this.

On a personal level, this is my favorite crystal. Almandine garnet is among the most beautiful substances on this planet. While it has some of the red that we associate with garnet, it also has hints of blue and green, white and black, yellow, and teal. In a lot of ways, that helps to give it a very intense aura. Unfortunately, this means this particular healing crystal can be too powerful for many people. It has elements of each of the categories that we've looked at, from wealth to love, to motivation and happiness. But almandine garnet can also bring with it some pain. This crystal has a way of making us look deeply at ourselves to see who we are. When we are living a life that doesn't align with our true selves, we are going to find ourselves experiencing pain and disappointment. This has stopped many people from using almandine garnet more than once, but it should be seen, not as a negative, but as a neutral. We wouldn't be upset with what was revealed if we lived our lives according to that deepest, truest version of ourselves. Using almandine garnet may make you feel disappointed, but if you take those lessons and act on them, then each subsequent session with almandine garnet will be much better. While this may not seem directly tied to courage or motivation, consider the way it helps encourage us to live as authentic a life as possible. The closer we get to that true self, the more courage we find in our actions and the fewer doubts we carry with us. Perhaps it is a roundabout way of getting to courage and motivation, but one that will pay dividends for the rest of your life when approached with the correct attitude.

Our final crystal for this section and this chapter is orange calcite. Sometimes called the Stone for Creativity, this crystal looks like a tangerine was turned into a stone. It comes to us exclusively from Mexico, making it one of the more rare crystals to get your hands on. Yet it has an aura that absolutely buzzes with motivation and a sense of unlimited potential. To hold a piece of orange calcite in your hand is to feel a connection to the power inside us. This crystal is primarily used to help promote creativity. It is highly recommended for artists, writers, filmmakers, and anyone else that works in a creative field, or who considers themselves to be an artist regardless of medium. Orange calcite also has amplification properties that will help to increase the effectiveness of the crystals it is used in conjunction with. If you are looking to tap into your motivation and keep going, then perform a lying down meditation, and place the orange calcite on your stomach just above your groin. This will keep it close to the sacral chakra and help to keep it open. If you have the option, adding a piece of orange calcite to your belt will allow you to keep it close to the sacral chakra throughout the day so that you can carry the benefits with you rather than having to take the time to tap into them in the morning or evening.

## Chapter Summary

- The most common use for healing crystals is to help us to remove negativity, invite positivity, and take control of our feelings.

- There are more than two hundred different types of crystals, which each has unique properties that we can benefit from.

- Anxiety and depression are crippling afflictions that can suck the joy out of life. While they should never be taken lightly, we can find help dealing with them through our crystals.

- Citrine is a powerful crystal that helps to remove negative energies from around us.

- Sunstone is a yellow and pink crystal that removes negativity and invites positivity.

- Smoky quartz crystals are very potent because they not only remove negativity, but they trap it inside of themselves. This requires them to be cleansed frequently, but it can do wonders for your mental health.

- Rose quartz is most strongly associated with love, but that love is also a sense of self-love, which is something we need in order to feel like we belong.

- Angel Aura is another type of quartz, though it has been treated with a metal to take on an iridescent quality. This is a very powerful crystal that beginners might want to avoid, but it can certainly help to ward off a negative mindset.

- Crystals with a common color tend to offer similar benefits. Yellow is associated with happiness, blue with relaxation, red and pink with love.

- Sodalite is a blue crystal that is so good at helping us to relax that it has been nicknamed the stone of peace.

- Kyanite is another blue and relaxing stone that can help you to feel more connected on a spiritual level.

- Shungite is a dark stone, but it helps to remove negative energies and can block EMF fields.

- Himalayan salt rock might sound more tasty than helpful, but it is high in vibrations and helps to burn away stress.

- Crystals for happiness include smoky quartz, as it removes negativity; rose quartz, for the self love promoting qualities; clear quartz, because it removes negativity and amplifies other crystals; citrine, which helps us to feel confident; amazonite, which works like citrine; amethyst, which promotes a sense of calm in the face of negativity.

- Crystals for love are most often pink or red, such as rose quartz, amber, garnet, rhodochrosite, rose tourmaline, and red agate.

- Lapis lazuli is also a profound crystal for attracting love, despite its blue appearance. This is true for opal as well.

- Crystals that attract wealth are often green. But we also see yellow crystals like citrine or tiger's eye are used for bringing wealth to us.

- Courage and motivation are necessary qualities if we want to live as fully as possible, yet sometimes they can feel like they are in short supply. Carnelian, ruby, blue apatite, yellow jasper, almandine garnet, and orange calcite are powerful crystals that can help you to find the motivation to keep going and achieve your hopes and dreams.

In the next chapter, you will learn about the crystals that are recommended for beginners. While anyone could grab a crystal and start from there, it is best to begin small and work your way up so that you have a sense of how each of these crystals functions and brings about an improvement in your life, your emotions, or your mental experience.

# CHAPTER THREE

# RECOMMENDED CRYSTALS FOR BEGINNERS

In the last chapter, while looking at crystals for healing specific emotions, we discussed how certain crystals weren't appropriate for beginners. Each crystal has a vibrational force that works to attract different energies to our lives. Sometimes these energies are positive and help to heal us from the detrimental effects of negativity. Other times these energies are used to open us up to creativity, wealth, love, passion, relaxation, motivation, and more. It should immediately be clear why we would want to bring these energies into our lives, but it is helpful to do it in a way in which you don't overwhelm yourself. This might be a little bit confusing to understand, so let's turn to a metaphor.

Ninety percent of the adult population in North America drinks coffee, so let's use this as a jumping-off point. If you prefer, pretend that we are talking about alcohol or beer, as these follow the same pattern as coffee. When you first are introduced to this delicious beverage, it can be quite overwhelming. A single cup can keep you up all hours of the night, and you may even experience muscle spasms. If you haven't had any coffee before, then you absolutely don't want to start with an espresso. But, if you have been drinking coffee for any length of time, then you know how quickly you get used to it. Then you can start drinking extra-strong or even espresso if you want. It will still have a much stronger kick than a regular cup of coffee, but it won't knock your socks off anymore. This is pretty much exactly what happens when we start using crystals. Those that are too powerful can be overwhelming and put us off of using crystals, just like an espresso taken early can make us not want to try coffee ever again. When you build up naturally, you increase your ability to handle the energies of even the strongest crystals.

In order to ensure that you don't jump in at the deep end, this chapter will briefly look at which crystals have an energy that isn't too intrusive for a beginner. You may want to go ahead and grab yourself a strong crystal such as almandine garnet, but you will find your experience to be far more pleasant if you take your time and build up your skill. It is better to build slowly than to burn out quickly, after all!

## Hematite

Hematite is used to promote a sense of stability within our emotions. Instead of being all over the place, with our emotions scattered to the winds, hematite helps us to find an island inside ourselves from which we can identify and witness our emotions. From this place, we are able to take much needed calming breaths that help us to remove negativity from our lives. Things like stress and anxiety can be let go of, and the hematite will trap them inside of itself, preventing them from returning to you.

The relaxation that hematite offers makes it a wonderful stone for those who feel like they are often under a lot of pressure. If you are a university student or someone working in a hectic industry, a piece of hematite should be kept nearby to remind you that you are more than your studies or your job. Even though there may be inevitable stresses, they shouldn't be allowed to ruin your mental and spiritual health.

Hematite has a gentle aura, which is ideal for beginners, as it creates a soothing feeling rather than a strong or overpowering one. It needs to be purified regularly to remove the toxic and negative energies that it absorbs. I believe that beginners should always have at least one crystal that requires them to perform a cleansing, as this is a crucial process and should be learned early. Many of the more advanced crystals that you will come to use need to be cleansed quite often, otherwise they can actually backfire and invite more negativity than they remove. Starting with a gentle stone like hematite will allow you to get used to cleansing without increasing the stakes in a large way. The more you can learn at this point, the better off you will be in the long run.

**Citrine**

We've seen citrine pop up several times throughout this book, and so it should be clear that this is one crystal that is extremely flexible in its uses. It can help you to stay motivated, it can help you to stay positive, it removes negative energy from your life, and it is even used to help attract wealth. Not only that, but it also has connections to fertility and creativity. With all of these disparate features, you might think that this crystal would be overly powerful.

And yet citrine is anything but. While it has an extensive range of possible uses and attracts lots of different energies, citrine is a very mild crystal with a subtle vibrational energy that makes it easy to use. If you could only select one crystal to begin with, you would be well advised to go with a piece of citrine.

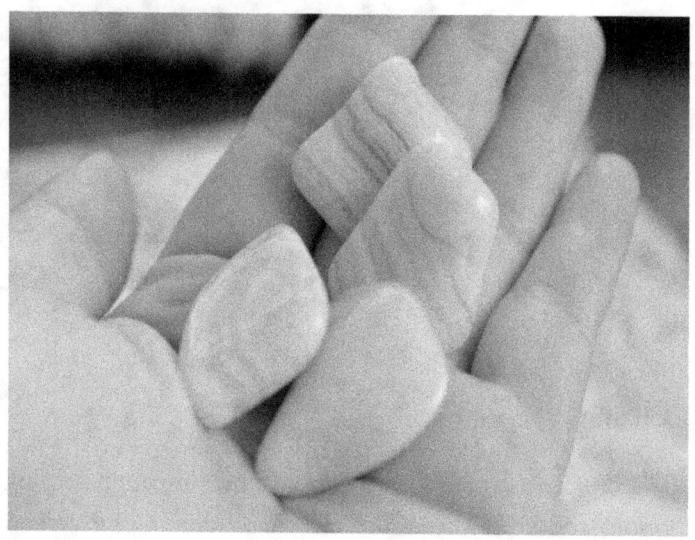

## Blue Lace Agate

We've looked at red agate, but, really, if you are going to begin with any type of agate, then it should be one of the blue lace variety. This crystal has a smooth texture and a light blue color that helps to promote a sense of calm. We've discussed the way that losing sight of your deeper, truest self can cause a lot of discomfort in life. Blue lace agate is one of the crystals for beginners that is great at helping to heal this divide and reconnect us to that self deep inside. Blue lace agate is used to help us to speak more openly and sincerely, both to ourselves and in our interactions with others.

Blue lace agate is among the best crystals to wear in a necklace, as it is usually strongly tied to the chakra in our throat that helps facilitate communication. If you are in a position in which you need to be a leader, or perhaps even just a public speaker, then a piece of blue lace agate worn around the neck can help to keep you speaking clearly and expressing nothing but your deepest truth.

## Clear Quartz

Among the many quartz crystals that we use for healing purposes, clear quartz is one of the strongest and yet also one of the best for beginners. Called the Master Healer, clear quartz is used to help us repair the damage from negativity, keep our aura clear from darkness, release negative emotions which have caused us pain, and even more. It is also one of the crystals which absorb negativity into itself so that it can't re-enter your life. What that means is you will need to learn to practice cleansing rituals so as to keep your clear quartz working at the highest level possible.

Clear quartz also acts as an amplifier. While it doesn't have a strong energy of its own, or, rather, an intrusive energy, clear quartz helps to boost the vibrations of the crystals around it. If used in a spread or a ritual, this can cause another weaker crystal to become much stronger. This is something that beginners need to be aware of. You may be using blue lace agate, for example, because it has a subtle power which makes it terrific for beginners, only to find that it becomes much more difficult to use once clear quartz is introduced. To address this, begin by using clear quartz on its own, and then slowly introduce other crystals into your practice, whether that be meditation, wearing crystal jewelry, or creating a crystal grid. It is always best to build up and introduce new crystals one at a time so that you can feel the difference and not overwhelm yourself in the process.

**Amethyst**

When you are feeling swamped by life, it is crucial that the crystal you use to help relax and ground you isn't itself overwhelming. This would only exacerbate the problem rather than help to solve it. Thankfully, amethyst is one of the best crystals for clearing the mind, plus one that is a great choice for beginners because of the gentle vibrations it emits. Amethyst also has protective properties that it uses to ward off negative energy that would otherwise seek to keep you down.

Meditation with amethyst will clear the mind and help boost our spiritual defenses. It can also be used in a grid, though it is important not to add too many crystals to a grid at once when you are beginning. Perhaps the most beneficial aspect of amethyst is the way that it helps to protect us in our sleep. Negative energies often try to get at us through our subconscious, and we see this manifest itself as nightmares. These can prevent us from getting refreshing sleep or even sometimes wake us up in the middle of the night. To prevent these negative energies from disturbing our rest, place a piece of amethyst under your pillow before bed so that you can benefit from the protection it offers.

## Pyrite

Known as fool's gold, pyrite is used to promote wealth and success in business. Keeping a piece of pyrite at your workspace can help you to achieve more, get a promotion, and invite healthy energy into the workspace, a place which may typically have a problem with attracting positivity. Another of the benefits that pyrite offers is a deep sense of confidence, which is fantastic for those that need to assert themselves in their jobs.

Where some crystals have a strong energy that can be overwhelming, pyrite has a strong energy that helps to improve your willpower. If you are finding yourself unable to get motivated or to push through work and deal with the other tasks you have on your plate, meditating with pyrite and keeping it nearby will help you to overcome these challenges.

# CRYSTALS FOR BEGINNERS

## Chapter Summary

- Despite the fact that all of the crystals we have discussed bring a positive force, these energies can be overwhelming if you aren't yet used to them.

- It is best to start with some crystals that have a more subtle vibration so that you can get used to them and build up your tolerance. You should also try starting with only one crystal at a time, getting used to it, and then moving onto another. In time, you can build up your skills to be able to deal with the energy from thousands of crystals at once.

- Hematite is a crystal that helps us find stability in our emotions, to relax when things are getting scary, and to remember that we aren't the situations we find ourselves in. Hematite has a gentle aura, though it works to amplify the crystals around it, so you should use it with caution.

- Citrine is a crystal for many purposes. Despite the fact that it can be used for so many different things, it has a very peaceful and subtle energy which makes it great for beginners. If you can only get one crystal to begin, get a citrine.

- Blue lace agate has a smooth texture and light blue color that help it to increase the sense of calm you feel when holding onto it. It is also used to help us speak more honestly, and so it benefits from being worn as a necklace so it can be close to the throat chakra.

- Clear quartz is a powerful crystal, often called the master healer because of the way it helps to heal our body, mind, and soul. The powerful aura that clear quartz has is great for helping us to get over the damage caused by negativity. It's important to note that clear quartz acts as an amplifier to increase the power of crystals nearby. This can make a subtle crystal turn into an overwhelming crystal, so use carefully.

- Amethyst is a fantastic crystal for relaxing and clearing your mind. It has protective properties and stops negative energy from getting you down. Beginners should try sleeping with a piece of amethyst under their pillow to ward off bad dreams.

- Pyrite, also known as fool's good, helps us succeed in business and find wealth. Of the crystals related to wealth, it is the most approachable for beginners who should consider keeping a piece near their workspace to benefit from the deep sense of confidence it provides.

In the next chapter, you will learn how to use your crystals. There are many different ways in which we can use them, but we'll be sticking with the most typical, as these easily make up 80% of how most people will want to employ them. The most common approach is to wear your crystals as jewelry, but their uses can differ widely. Some use their crystals for home decor, others sleep with them to get their benefits, while they're unconscious, and others meditate with their crystals, or use them in various rituals. When it comes to using them, always follow your heart and intuition. The crystals themselves will generally provide a guide to what's right for you.

# CHAPTER FOUR

# HOW TO USE HEALING CRYSTALS

While looking at individual crystals, we have discussed some of the ways in which they are best used. These have mostly covered meditation or wearing them as jewelry. These are certainly the two most common ways to use crystals, and as such, they will each be discussed in this chapter, but they are far from being the only ways. We'll be looking at how we can use crystals in ways ranging from meditation to bathing, drinking to sleeping, and from gardening to jewelry. We'll even make a few more stops between each of these, as there really are just so many different methods for you to utilize your crystals.

If you are unsure of what the best approach is, then you should start simple with meditation or jewelry. Both of these methods can significantly improve your life as you tap into the energy inside of your crystals, and, in time, they will help you to grow comfortable enough to branch out and experiment with other applications. All the variations that you find in this book are potent, and there isn't a single method that is right or wrong. It all depends on what is best for you, and only you have the power to make that decision. When dealing with energies such as these, your intuition and gut-feeling are more important than anything I could ever tell you. With that said, let's look at the many ways in which people have put these amazing tools to use.

## Meditation

Among all of the ways of using your crystals, meditation is by far the most powerful. This is because meditation itself is a powerful tool. Often considered as part of the Buddhist belief system, meditation doesn't have to be necessarily thought of as a religious or spiritual practice. For many people, it can be a way of getting in touch with their spiritual self, but just as many others meditate because science has shown that it is one of the most beneficial practices for health. It helps us to calm down, reduce our stress levels, boost our happiness, and increase our life expectancy. All of these bonuses come when we meditate, whether we're using a crystal or not. But if we add a crystal to our meditation and use it as our point of focus, we are able to achieve much more out of this practice. If you haven't meditated before, don't worry. It isn't that hard, and adding a crystal to your practice is very simple.

Let's begin by looking at meditation itself. There is a misconception that meditation is the act of sitting down and clearing our minds. This may happen when we meditate, but it isn't actually how meditation works. That's important to remember because I have encountered many people who say they can't meditate because their minds are too active. Ironically, by saying that they are putting the finger on their problem. It is exactly these people who need meditation the most. When we meditate, we often do manage to clear our minds, but this is a byproduct of meditation rather than meditation itself. Plus, when we practice meditation properly, we increase our ability to clear our minds and focus on a single thing at a time. This helps to improve how well we focus on the other elements in our lives, such as the work we have on hand.

To meditate, find somewhere comfortable to sit or lie down. Some practices, especially Buddhist practices, are very specific about the posture of the body during meditation. If you are just starting, don't worry too much about this. Just find a position that is comfortable for you to stay in for ten minutes. Close your eyes and take a deep breath through your nose. Hold it for five to seven seconds, then slowly let it go out of your mouth. Repeat this. That is all basic meditation is. People think that they are supposed to sit down and clear their minds, but this isn't the case. All you need to do is focus on your breathing. You may find that your mind begins to wander, and you might even consider this to mean you have failed. But as soon as you realize that your attention has wandered, you bring it back to your breathing. It is through the act of bringing your attention back to your breathing that you make it easier to focus further down the road. It can seem counter-intuitive, having to lose your focus in order to develop it, but this is the same thing that happens when we are learning new information. When we try to remember something, we often think that having a hard time remembering it is a bad sign. But if you are learning a new topic, it is the act of struggling to remember that makes it easier. By going through our minds to find the information, we make the information take a stronger hold. Thus, by losing our focus and then returning it, we make it easier for us to keep our focus in the future.

So, as a general guideline, that is how you meditate. Now, let's add a crystal to the practice.

Rather than focusing on your breathing, when meditating with a crystal, you focus on the crystal. This is easiest done when you focus on the physical feeling of the crystal. For example, some people like to lie down and place a crystal on their forehead. This practice is primarily used to strengthen your third eye or psychic tendencies. Another way is to hold your crystal in your hand, or even to hold a different crystal in each hand. Rub your thumb over the crystal and really concentrate on the way that it feels. You shouldn't have to open your eyes this way, although you can if you want to. Opening your eyes when meditating isn't recommended because the visual senses can easily break you out of your concentration. When meditating traditionally, we focus on the feeling on the rise and fall of the chest and the cold, crisp feeling of the oxygen as it fills our lungs. When we meditate with a crystal, we replace this feeling with that of the crystal itself. It is important to have this physical feeling because it is through focusing on this that the brain begins to quiet down the regions not necessary to maintain the focus. It is this act of quieting that people think is meditation itself, not just the result thereof.

When we meditate with a crystal, we carefully select the crystal we are going to use based on the attributes that we are looking to invite into our lives. If we are looking for love, then we would meditate with a rose tourmaline or another love-focused crystal. For wealth, we might meditate with a piece of jade. Rather than focusing on the crystal's intentions, we focus on the physical aspect of the crystal and let the intention naturally come out and fill us up. When we try to focus too much on the intention, we get lost in our minds as we consider things like the reason we choose that intention. The reason isn't crucial; what is important is narrowing your focus and opening yourself up as widely as possible. This can't happen when we're running through our minds and unintentionally bringing in extraneous emotions to the session. You may want to take a few minutes prior to meditation to focus on the intention, but once you are meditating, all of that needs to be let go of and set aside until after you have finished.

Meditation is best done once or twice a day. It is recommended to meditate in the morning before the day gets fully started. Doing this is great for our mental health, but it is even better when meditating with crystals as it allows us to tap into their energies before anything happens in the day. The longer we wait, the more issues we risk encountering. For example, if you go about your day and continue to get stressed out, then you will probably turn to meditation with a relaxing crystal. But if you begin the day by meditating with a calming crystal, you are far less likely to let that would-be stress affect you in the first place. Starting early is always recommended. Likewise, it is also recommended that you pay attention to getting restful sleep at night. While you are unconscious, your brain is still pumping away and living. It uses this time to make sense of the day and to defuse harmful energies. If we are bringing negative energies with us to sleep, then they can make this experience lousy, filled with nightmares or tossing and turning. But a meditation before bed helps to protect ourselves from these energies and invite more positivity into the experience. Meditating twice a day might seem like a lot, but it's only 20 minutes, far less time than we waste checking social media or scrolling through the channels of the TV. Plus, if you are tight on time, it is good to know that as little as two minutes a day can have a positive effect on your life. You can also set the intentions for your crystals before getting home or while you are in the shower so that you can jump right into the meditation without wasting any time.

## Carrying Crystals

The easiest way to use your crystals is to carry them with you throughout your day. This might seem too easy, but it can have a surprisingly powerful effect. To get the most out of our crystals, we need to attune to them and develop a relationship with them. When you first buy a crystal, it will bring in energy to your life, but it is kind of like trying to fit a square peg in a round hole. You might get some of the potency out of it, but there is a lot more that isn't helping you yet. But as you spend more time with your crystals, you start to create a much better fit. It's as though the edges of that square peg have been worn down so that now it's a round peg that fits perfectly into a round hole. We aren't literally wearing away any part of us or our crystals, but the metaphor gets the idea across.

You can toss a crystal into a purse and still get some benefit, but it is better to keep it closer to yourself. A breast pocket is the best, but the pocket in your pants is also a good fit. If you are using a crystal that is associated with the heart chakra, then you should use the breast pocket or consider wearing a necklace that allows the crystal to hang over your heart. You can still put one of these crystals into a pants pocket, but it won't be as effective. Crystals associated with the sacral chakra are better off in your pants compared to around your neck, so it is all about putting the specific crystal as close as possible to the chakra it's intended to open.

With that said, if you don't have a way to keep a heart chakra crystal near your heart, then don't feel like there is any reason not to take it with you in a pocket. It is far better to have it on your person rather than leaving it at home. This is especially true if you are heading out to face a tough experience or one that causes you nervousness. You can always reach into your pocket to feel the crystal and tap into its positive energies for courage, strength, or whatever you are looking to gain from it.

## Drinking a Crystal Elixir

Out of all the possible ways of using crystals, this is the one that could hurt you the most. Before we even get into how to make a crystal elixir, we need to talk about the possible risks. There are some crystals that are toxic when consumed. For example, amazonite is poisonous and could cause a lot of bodily harm if ingested.

Furthermore, there are crystals such as celestite, which can break apart or degrade when put into liquid. Before making a crystal elixir, you should always take the time to open up Google and search, "Is [crystal] safe for use in an elixir?" That will give you an idea if there are any health concerns you need to be aware of. Make sure you consult with reliable and reputable sources before proceeding with your elixir. With that said, we'll look now at what a crystal elixir is, how to make one, and how we can make one with a toxic crystal without in any way risking our health.

A crystal elixir is one of the ways we can get as close as possible to our crystals and the energies that they contain. Rather than keeping those energies outside of ourselves and requiring them to pass through our bodies from the outside in, we can infuse water with crystal so that we can literally ingest the energy from the crystal so that it fills up our bodies from the inside. This process can be quite powerful, and beginners should start with one of the crystals recommended in chapter three, and only after they've spent time getting used to that crystal's particular vibrations. However, if you believe that you are in control of your relationship with your crystal, and not likely to be overwhelmed, then making a crystal elixir can be like making crystal energy drinks. Instead of caffeine and wakefulness, you create a drink which helps to fill you up with the positive properties of your chosen crystal.

To begin with, you need to cleanse it. Even if you have just purchased a new one for yourself, you should cleanse it before using it anyway, let alone using it to make a crystal elixir. We'll cover cleansing in the next chapter. For now, let us assume that you have properly cleansed the crystal you are looking to use in your elixir. The next step is to fill a container up with fresh water. This is best done with spring water that doesn't have any chemicals added to it for cleaning purposes. If you have access to well water, then this will work, but it's advisable to avoid using tap water, as you can't be sure what is in it. Next, place your crystal into the water. There are two camps as to what to do now. One camp sees this as the point in which you drink the water, with the crystal still in it. But the other viewpoint, which I recommend, suggests leaving the crystal in the water overnight to soak. In the morning, you can remove the crystal and choose to drink the elixir then. Or you can store it in the fridge to make it last longer. I like to mix up a big batch in a juice pitcher so that I can fill my water bottle several times. I also tend to have two pitchers of crystal elixir or more in my fridge at a time so that I can choose the right type of drink to help me with whatever it is I happen to be going through that day.

As mentioned above, not every crystal is fit for making a crystal elixir this way. Those that would cause us harm should not be ingested in any way. But this doesn't mean that we can make elixirs using them, just that we have to be careful. If you want to make a crystal elixir using a crystal like amazonite, you should get yourself a container with a top like a mason jar. Fill the jar up with water and then put the top on. Sit the crystal on top of the lid and keep it there overnight. In the morning, you have yourself a crystal elixir without any risk of causing harm. This elixir won't be as powerful as one that can soak directly, but it is still quite effective.

You should note that there are water bottles that you can buy, which are designed to have a crystal placed in them. These are often quite expensive, though they are very beautiful, and they make it easy to create a crystal elixir. But in no way should you feel like you have to invest in one of these. You could make a crystal elixir in a mason jar, a juice jug, or even a pot of water if it was all you had. Just make sure that you use cleansed crystals and, when using toxic crystals, make sure they have no direct contact with the water you're drinking.

**Bathing**

One of the best ways to use relaxing crystals is to add them to your bath. Just like with crystal elixirs, you should be careful not to add toxic crystals into your bath water as these toxins can be absorbed through the skin and cause lots of damage to your body. You should also avoid using crystals like pyrite as pyrite turns into sulfuric acid when combined with water, and I can't think of anything less relaxing than an acid bath! But, so long as the crystal is safe to add to water, then you may want to place it directly into the bath. Those crystals which can't be added to the bath can be kept on the ledge of the tub or nearby so as to offer their energy to the room.

Bathrooms are often the smallest rooms we have in our houses, so keep in mind how tight the space is when you are preparing for a crystal bath. The more crystals you bring into the space, the more energy you are bringing in, and this can quickly become overwhelming. Taking a bath is one of the worst places to have a feeling of being overwhelmed. The bath is so comfortable you don't feel like getting out to move the crystals, but the overwhelming feeling prevents us from fully enjoying ourselves. Nothing is more disappointing than getting out of the bath and feeling as tight and wound up as we did when we first sat down.

If you are mindful of what crystals you use and what energy they bring, then taking a crystal bath can be one of the more relaxing experiences of your life. Consider bringing in crystals on the blue spectrum, as these tend to have the most calming vibrations. Of course, you don't necessarily need to take a bath to soothe yourself. It can be an intimate and bonding experience to bathe with a lover, and a bath of this sort could benefit from red, love-oriented crystals rather than those with an aura of relaxation. A bath can also be a fantastic way to meditate, so you may want to bring in crystals to promote wealth, health, happiness, motivation, or more.

Keep in mind the way that the various energies change the feeling of the bath. Start with only one crystal at a time until you are comfortable enough to bring in several as you relax in the water.

**Crystal Grid**

Creating a crystal grid is one form of ritual that we can perform with our crystals. As such, it's helpful that you stick to what you feel inside when working with them. There are some suggestions that you can find online for how to make a crystal grid, such as arranging your crystals in a circular pattern, but if you want to amplify the energy of your crystals as much as possible, then you should follow your instincts and arrange them as you see fit.

To perform a crystal grid ritual, you must start with an end goal in mind. This initial step is something that we will be looking at more in detail in the next chapter. For now, take a moment to figure out what it is you want. Perhaps you are trying to let go of some unhappiness or anger. Maybe you are trying to attract romantic love into your life. Whatever the reason that drives you, make sure that you understand it and have it mind when you start. Next, select crystals that have an energy that supports this desire. How many crystals you choose is up to you; just remember that beginners should start with fewer crystals and slowly work their way up by adding a new one only after getting used to the energy of those they're working with. It can be easy to blow out and create a negative feeling when we are inundated with the power of our crystals.

Once you have selected those crystals which will make up your grid, start to arrange them in front of you. You can place them however you like, based on a pattern that you've seen before or simply place them where it feels right. When you are starting, the chances are that you will be placing the crystals on this instinctual basis, and that will be all the meaning that each placement holds. But as you work more often with crystal grids, you will see the way you can invest extra meaning in the particular spots that you place them. This is similar to the way that a tarot card spread assigns a specific meaning to each spot. When you start to define spaces in your grid, you are able to control the way that the energies are flowing together in a more minute fashion. This can have a telling effect and be very significant, so don't worry about assigning meaning to each space until after you have already made a few crystal grids.

While it is called a *crystal* grid, there is no reason that you can't bring in other objects. Some people like to bring in seashells and other naturally occurring objects. Others will use items that have a particular meaning to them like a wedding ring or even a stuffed toy animal. You can bring in anything you want, so long as you understand what the item means to you because the meaning will greatly affect the energies you are working with. Also, keep in mind that, while you want to select crystals which support your intention, your grid can benefit from adding some crystals that help to amplify the power of the other crystals around it. So you might choose an intention which isn't strongly connected to clear quartz, but choose clear quartz to be a part of the grid anyway as it will reinforce the others.

After you make your crystal grid, you will want to leave it be for a while. Consider it almost like cooking an elaborate dish. You need to get all the ingredients together first to cook the dish, but before it can be served, it needs to sit for a little while so that everything falls into place. The energies from the crystals aren't going to gel together immediately. They need to be given a chance to co-habitat the same space and to settle in. Once they have, there will be a concrete and solid energy that is palpable. So don't expect a crystal grid to immediately start producing power the moment you add the last crystal. You need to remember to be patient. The power is growing.

**Taking Them to Bed**

We've seen a couple of different crystals that help us to ward off nightmares. You might think that is the only benefit to taking crystals with you to bed, but if you believe that, then you are cutting yourself off from a lot of potential positive energy that could help improve your life. We spend between seven to nine hours in bed every single day. For many of us, it is the most enjoyable part of the day. But it is also the least productive, as it is hard to achieve much when we're off in Neverland. Yet we could be leveling up our sleep by using crystals.

As with making a crystal grid, you want to consider your intentions before picking a crystal to bring to bed. If you are dealing with a lot of anxiety, then you might want to bring a smoky quartz or another of the crystals which help to remove toxic negativity from your life. But if you aren't dealing with anxiety, and, instead, you want to attract romantic love, then the smoky quartz wouldn't be nearly as effective as a rose quartz. By choosing the intention, you can ensure that you are promoting the most effective use of your sleep and absorbing positive energies.

Just like how we benefit from carrying crystals with us, we benefit from being close to them at night when we sleep. You can place a crystal on your nightstand, or even create a crystal grid and place it on your nightstand (though please take your time to build up to this). But for the best effect, you should put the crystal underneath your pillow. The under-the-pillow approach is doubly beneficial if you choose a crystal that is linked to the crown chakra on the top of your head. That isn't to say you won't feel the effects of a crystal that is linked to the root or sacral chakra when it is placed under your pillow, just that it is more effective the closer you can keep the associated chakra.

## Make Jewelry

It is undeniable that there are many people who think that healing crystals are silly. Whether this comes from a place of fear, envy, or ignorance, the reality is that it can be very annoying or even painful to have someone call you out for your beliefs. This is much more likely to happen if someone sees you creating a grid, meditating with a crystal, or the like. But the beauty of these crystals helps to show our belief loud and clear without drawing attention to it. Simply put, we can make jewelry out of our crystals. When you are wearing a necklace or a bracelet with a gorgeous crystal in it, you are more likely to have people ask you where you got it rather than insult your personal beliefs. Just wait to see the look on their face when you tell them that you made it yourself!

You don't have to make your own jewelry, of course. There are plenty of options available to get jewelry that integrates healing crystals. But when you make it yourself, there is a much stronger bond to both the crystals (as you chose the exact ones to include), as well as a sentimental value attached to it as a piece of jewelry. There are many guides online that aim to teach you how to make jewelry, and it is very easy to incorporate healing crystals into these tutorials. Plus, they are an absolute blast! There is such a sense of pride and joy that comes from making something yourself that you would be denying yourself a lot of happiness if you decided to skip out and just purchase a pre-made one. However, there is no shame at all in purchasing a piece of jewelry that has already been made. You still gain a wonderful piece of jewelry; it's just you don't get that feeling of pride that comes from the act of creation.

Healing crystal jewelry is also one of the best ways for us to get our crystals as close as possible to their corresponding chakra. We can create tiaras for our highest chakras, chokers for the neck, and necklaces to dangle down over our hearts. We can add healing crystals to a belt to get closer to the sacral and root. Or we can wear crystals in bracelets or anklets. This is a major plus that jewelry has over simply carrying our crystals with us.

Be careful about one thing when making your healing crystal jewelry. I know it's been repeated to death, but you don't want to mix too many crystals until you are used to their energies. You might think it looks lovely to have five different crystals all on the same necklace, but then if the energy is overwhelming, you might find that wearing the necklace makes you feel like you are choking. When you first begin, start with jewelry that only has a single healing crystal. Next, you can add two more once you are used to them. You might want to try amplifying your original piece. Let's say you have a rose quartz necklace. Instead of adding more crystals to further the love energy, try adding a couple of clear quartz crystals that could amplify the strength of the original crystal. It is my suggestion that you first amplify your crystal before you alter the jewelry by adding other crystals to it.

**Block Electromagnetic Fields**

Everything that is alive produces an electromagnetic field. It is this field that gives us life, that allows us to think. There is a very surreal realization to be had when you start to look into electromagnetic fields, and you realize that we, as human beings, are continuously producing an electrical wave. We talk about "neurons firing" in our brains when we mean we are thinking about something or connecting ideas. It is almost crazy to realize that these thoughts, this firing, is an electric one. We are able to think because we create electromagnetic responses within ourselves.

But, it turns out, this also comes at a cost. Our modern society produces more electromagnetic fields than ever before. There are radio waves, cellular signals, and we are always looking at either a television, computer, or phone screen, and each of these devices produces an electromagnetic field. This is quite harmful to us. Consider the game of telephone that you played as a child. A message was whispered in one person's ear. That person would whisper to the next person, and it would go all around the classroom until it got back to the first person, at which point the message was so different as to be unrecognizable. The chaos of the game telephone is reflective of the chaos that happens to us when we're exposed to so many electromagnetic fields. Our thoughts have a harder time forming and coming together because there is so much interference between them due to outside forces.

There is still much research to be done regarding these fields, but many scientists believe they aren't healthy for us. Whether they contribute to the skyrocketing levels of anxiety in our modern society, or to physical poor health and illness, only time will tell. But enough has been explored on the topic to make even the bravest soul a little bit nervous once they start digging into it. Thankfully, some healing crystals are thought to have the ability to block out these electromagnetic fields and help us to remove ourselves from their onslaught. Malachite, black tourmaline, and shungite are just a few of the crystals which are considered to have this capability.

Blocking these fields is thankfully quite simple. Just purchase one of the crystals with these EMF blocking properties, and place them by any of the electronics in your house like your television or computer monitor. If people are right about these properties, then this is a way of protecting yourself from the harmful fields. If they are wrong, well, then you still have a beautiful looking crystal in your home as part of the decor. Plus, you can always use that crystal in a grid or add it to a piece of jewelry later on if you so choose.

**Decoration**

While you might think that this goes without saying, these crystals can make for wonderful decorations. They can add color to a room, and they can be used together or alone to create delightful highlights in any location in your house. While many people use crystals exactly for this reason, you shouldn't think that crystal decorations are simply pretty, and that's all. Remembering that these crystals have forceful energies, we need to be mindful of the way that they change the natural energy of the room. One of the reasons that crystals are often used for decoration is to promote a better sense of feng shui in a room, and this is certainly one amazing use, but to dig deep into feng shui would take a book all of its own. Here we will content ourselves with speaking about general decorations.

Each room in your house has its vibration. A large part of this comes from the way that we invest personal energies into our living space. Using my quarters as an example, I have a kitchen, a bedroom, a living room, an office, and a bathroom. The bedroom has a relaxing energy, one that invites me to get a much deeper sleep than if I just laid down on the couch in the living room. The living room itself is relaxing, but there is a stronger sense of excitement and motion there, as I often entertain my guests there. In the kitchen, I have worked hard to create a sense of experimentation and play; it has a more random energy in which it feels like anything could happen at any moment. The office has a very focused and purposeful feeling, while the bathroom actually doesn't have much of an energy at all. These energies arise naturally from the way that I use and think about these rooms. I've also tried to promote my desired energy through the use of decorative crystals.

I have creative crystals in the kitchen, specifically tangerine quartz and Herkimer diamond. I have blue quartz and blue tiger's egg in the office. Amethyst and labradorite in the bedroom. Rose quartz, clear quartz, and amethyst round out the living room. I don't keep these crystals next to each other, as I prefer to spread them out to create almost a Venn diagram of energy in each room. But I have specifically chosen then for the vibrations that they promote. They look beautiful, and I have often received compliments on them, though my friends complimenting them didn't realize that I was using them for their energies. They simply saw a decoration that struck them as attractive. This is great, as there are several of my friends who would laugh if I told them the underlying purpose. Yet, I feel their comments are the clearest sign that it is working.

When deciding how to use crystals to decorate your home, start by considering what you want each room to promote. Happiness, love, lust, relaxation, creativity, all of these are valid choices, and they should be picked depending on your personal desires. Just because I like to have a relaxing energy in my bedroom doesn't mean you have to. You might be better suited by putting romantic or seductive crystals in your bedroom. It is entirely up to you, but you do need to figure out what you want ahead of time.

Once you know what you want to promote, it is time for the best part: setting up your decorative crystals. You may want to combine multiple crystals to form decorations, though you should have experience using multiple crystals at once before you do so. Or, you might do what I do and space them out to create a more even distribution of energy. Whatever you pick, simply keep your intentions in mind as you build or display your decorations. When you are mindful of the energy that the decorations are bringing, you are able to really, truly control the way that your home feels, and make it much more in line with your true self.

## Chapter Summary

- Crystals make for powerful additions to a meditation session. You may want to hold your crystal, place it over one of your chakras, or stare at it as you meditate.

- Prior to meditating, figure out an intention that you want to bring into your life. This intention will help to pull energy from the crystal to infuse your life with its healing abilities.

- It is best to meditate twice a day to get the optimum effects.

- We can carry crystals with us throughout the day to benefit from their energy.

- When carrying crystals, it is best to keep them as close to ourselves as possible. Putting a crystal in a breast pocket is more effective than sticking it in your purse.

- Crystal elixirs are drinks that have been infused with the properties of a crystal. Be careful when making a crystal elixir, as some crystals are toxic, others dissolve in water, and yet others change form and become dangerous chemicals when introduced to water.

- You should always cleanse your crystals before using them as part of a crystal elixir.

- To make a crystal elixir, stick your chosen crystal into a bottle, cup, bowl, or pitcher of water and let it sit for a while. Then drink it when you are ready.

- You can use toxic crystals to make a crystal elixir, but they shouldn't be placed directly in the water. Instead, use a can or jar that has a lid and set the crystal on top of the lid. Let it stay that way overnight, as the lack of contact makes it take longer for the water to absorb the crystal's properties.

- Adding crystals to your bath can be an amazing method to create a more relaxing or meaningful experience. Be careful not to select crystals that are toxic. You could line the tub with them or have them nearby.

- You can combine a crystal bath with meditation for impressive results.

- A crystal grid is a pattern that you make with your crystals. The crystals work together to combine their energy and make a lasting effect. You need to leave a crystal grid to sit for several hours to let the vibrations properly align and mesh with each other.

- When making a crystal grid, let the crystals guide you to where they should be placed. Some people will tell you how they think a crystal grid should be done, but this is a personal opinion and not a set-in-stone rule.

- We often spend eight or more hours asleep every night. We can make productive use of this time by setting crystals on the nightstand or under our pillows so that their energies will infuse our lives while we sleep.

- Making jewelry is a great way to keep your crystals on you without drawing attention to your beliefs. Plus, there is a sense of pride that comes with creating something beautiful.

- Crystal jewelry is one of the easiest ways to keep our crystals close to the chakra that they are most associated with.

- Electromagnetic fields from devices are all around us, and they may well be harmful. Certain crystals are thought to help block out these fields to keep us safe. Simply place one of the blocking crystals next to your electronics.

- Crystals make for lovely decorations, but we should consider their placement carefully. We can set them out as decorations in such a fashion as to bring a positive or desired energy into the room.

- Crystals that are used as energy-inviting decorations should still be cleansed at least once a month.

In the next chapter, you will learn all sorts of tips that you can put to use to maximize your experience with your healing crystals. From techniques like combining crystals through to adding them into your daily routine, we'll cover everything you need to know in order to use your crystals like a pro.

# CHAPTER FIVE

# TIPS TO MAXIMIZE YOUR HEALING CRYSTALS

As we approach the end of the book, it might be helpful if we take a few minutes to consider some tips for maximizing the abilities and effectiveness of our healing crystals. We have briefly mentioned a few of these tips, and there is one that I hope you are already tired of hearing. But this chapter gathers these tips together to ensure that you leave with them fresh in your mind.

Even more than the tips we look at, you should pay special attention to the section on cleansing your crystals. If you are using them to remove negative energy from you, then nine times out of ten, this is going to be achieved by the crystal soaking up that negativity. If you don't cleanse the crystal, it will go bad and, instead of repelling negativity, it will invite that negativity. Obviously, this is the exact opposite of what we want, and so it is essential that you take this to heart and make sure you cleanse your crystals on a regular basis. You may choose to do this weekly, or you might fit the schedule to the phases of the moon. Pick the approach that is right for you. Speaking of right for you, that brings up to our first tip.

**Let the Crystals Choose You**

This particular tip is a little bit confusing because it contradicts other advice. Often when we go into the store or look to purchase crystals for the first time, we are best off going with one or two of the crystals that we looked at in chapter three. These have a more subtle energy that has a far smaller chance of swamping us. If we have never worked with energy before, these crystals are a great way to get started. But this isn't always the case. Sometimes, we are actually better advised to pick a strong crystal. The determining factor of which crystals are right for you isn't going to be anything that I have written here today, but rather it is going to be what you feel in your heart.

When you first look for crystals, you should try to open yourself up and be receptive to the vibrations that they are producing. This is best achieved in person. In fact, if you are only able to purchase your crystals online, then you should 100% stick to those listed in chapter three. But if you are able to purchase them in person, then try following these steps. Start by meditating before you go into the store. This doesn't need to be a long session, and, if need be, you can get away with taking a few deep breaths when you're on the sidewalk outside. The point of this is to take a moment to let your mind relax and open you up to the energy you are about to feel. More than anything else, this step is significant because the store you are about to enter is going to be bursting with energy, and you want to make sure that you are ready for that experience. When you aren't, you may find that the store spikes your anxiety or makes you feel deeply uncomfortable. Remember, this isn't the store itself, but the energies that are infused throughout it.

Next, once you have prepared yourself, enter into the store and navigate over to the crystals. You may have one or two that you intend to buy. Let yourself get these, but don't just go to the counter and rush off right away. Instead, take a few minutes to browse through the crystals available for purchase. You may want to reach your hand out and touch them or hover over them and be receptive to the way they make you feel. In all things to do with such energies, it is these feelings which should guide you first and foremost. If you feel compelled towards one of the crystals, then buy that one. It doesn't matter if it is the strongest crystal in that store. If your energy aligns with the crystal's energy, then you should go ahead and get it. Some of us are naturally drawn to certain powers. These energies might make another beginner sick, yet they fill you with a sense of purpose, calm, or connection.

Some people might argue that this could be dangerous. This is true; it can't be denied. It's possible for people to trick themselves into thinking they are more powerful than they are. Perhaps our vanity is providing unreliable advice. As part of your meditation beforehand, try to address your own sense of power and to approach the crystals the way that a newborn approaches the world. Try not to think of yourself as powerful. Instead, tell yourself that you have no power. This will help you to let go of your ego, which often tries to lead us down dangerous paths. Just keep in mind that this meditation is only for just before purchasing your crystal. After you get home, even before you use the crystals, take another moment to meditate for five or ten minutes. Instead of telling yourself anything, simply focus on your breathing and letting go of the earlier messages you told yourself. The truth is that you are powerful, even if that power isn't the kind necessary to use stronger crystals. Each of us has a power inside. We need to deny it and shut ourselves off from it if we want to open ourselves up to crystals for the first time, but to tell ourselves this throughout the day or, indeed, our life would be detrimental.

By letting the crystal choose you, you ensure that you are working with energies that flow naturally through you. That will reduce the amount of discomfort you feel when working with these healing crystals for the first time.

Keep in mind that you should also let the crystals pick the best approaches for their use. Sometimes we have specific uses for our crystals, such as meditation or decoration, but often we use the same crystals for several different purposes. You might carry a crystal in your pocket, use it as part of a grid later, and then create a crystal elixir with it at the end of the day. If you know that you want to work with a specific crystal, but you aren't sure to what end you should use it, consult the crystal. Hold it in your hand and see how it makes you feel. It will be able to suggest the most appropriate way of using it and benefiting from the vibrational powers it holds.

## Start Slow, Add More in Time

It has been mentioned again and again, but it is so important that it deserves to have its own section in this chapter. When you first get your hands on your crystals, you are going to want to make all sorts of different spreads. If you are looking to benefit from their energies, there is a high chance you are going to use them in conjunction with one another. This is something that we do when working with healing crystals, but it is something that we need to build up to and embrace slowly.

When we try to use too many crystals at once, we become overwhelmed, and we can experience unhappy results. This happens when we severely mess up our own energy. The result is confusion, depression, anxiety, a sense of things not being right, but without a clear cause. It isn't until we sit and we meditate and properly realign our chakras that we realize it was our energy that was the problem. It is easy to think that perhaps we are stressed out due to work, love, family, money. But these are all external causes when the real cause was coming from inside of us.

In the last section, we saw that it can be okay sometimes to go with a strong crystal early. You absolutely should not be combing a strong crystal like this with another until you are quite experienced with your crystals. But even if you go with a more subtle crystal for beginners, you shouldn't be combing these together. That is a recipe for disaster you don't want to cook up.

It can be hard to be patient, especially when we live in a society with a 24/7 news cycle, online shopping, and instant messaging. But crystals aren't subject to modern fashions, and they shouldn't be rushed. Please, use these with caution and take your time. It is better to go too slow than to go too fast. Consider it like a car. If you crash going 10 miles an hour, then you are going to be okay. If you crash at 100 miles an hour, then you are much more likely to suffer injury or worse. When it comes to "driving" our crystals, we want to start slow before we ramp up the speed.

**Cleanse Your Crystals Often and Thoroughly**

As mentioned above, we need to cleanse our crystals to keep them working at their best. The first time that we cleanse our crystals should be as soon as we get them home from the store. Then we'll want to purify them regularly or after we use them, depending on what we are using them for. For example, crystals should be cleansed prior to being used to make a crystal elixir. Healing crystals worn as jewelry, carried throughout the day, or used as decoration should be cleansed at least once a month, though it is better to go for twice a month if you can.

The reason for this is these crystals often don't just create energy, they also absorb it. So if we want to keep a crystal positive, we need to get rid of the negativity that it has absorbed. You may choose to cleanse your crystals in certain ways. For example, you might group together red crystals to cleanse one way, but cleanse blue crystals another. Below are several different ways that you can cleanse your crystals, but there isn't one that is especially better than another. As with choosing your crystals, it is best to let the crystal inform the purifying ritual that is right for it. With that in mind, the first two cleansing rituals we'll look at are far and away the most popular.

For an easy way to cleanse your crystal, use natural water. It is important to avoid using water that has been processed or bottled. You may be able to use tap water, but if you have a nearby stream, lake, or pond, then this water will be much more effective. It would also be terrific if you have access to well water. But the best possible choice, if it is an option, is to use rain as it is coming down. We aren't always able to do this since we should be cleansing our crystals often, and sometimes the rain seems like it is never going to come. But if you see that it is raining, this can be a terrific time for an impromptu cleansing session. Simply take your crystal outside and let it sit in the rain for ten minutes. If you don't have the option of using rain, then use one of the other sources of water for ten to fifteen minutes. Keep in mind that the stronger the flow of water, the less fitting it is for use with brittle crystals that could be damaged. If you are looking to cleanse a fragile crystal, then you're better suited with this next approach.

Both sunlight and moonlight can be used to cleanse a crystal. Of the two, sunlight could potentially damage the crystal and cause it to lose or change color. The result of that could be detrimental to the crystal's power, so make sure that you research your crystal to see if it is safe for sunlight. If not, that's okay. As it turns out, moonlight is much more powerful than sunlight when it comes to cleansing. If you are going to use the light of the moon to cleanse your crystals, wait until the moon is full. A full moon is a source of great power, and its beams will help to clean out your crystals and keep them working to their full potency, without the risk of discoloration.

If you are looking to cleanse a crystal that is connected with the earth, then you can use earth itself as a way of cleansing it. Black tourmaline, citrine, malachite, rose quartz, smoky quartz, and rhodochrosite are just a few of the crystals that can be cleansed in this manner. To purify a crystal using earth, go out into the backyard and carefully bury them. The energy of the earth will detoxify the crystal, though you need to consider the timing of this particular ritual carefully. You will want to leave the crystals in the earth for at least 24 hours, though they will benefit from longer stretches. Bear in mind that means that you will be without those crystals and so you can't rely on their energy should you need it.

For those crystals that are connected to fire, such as fire agate, aventurine, calcite, or garnet, you can purify them with fire. You need to be extremely careful when using fire for a cleansing ritual, as it can be easy to harm yourself if you aren't careful. You want the crystals to benefit from direct connection with the fire so that any negativity that has been trapped inside of them can be burnt away. While the smoke from the fire itself has some cleansing attributes, and your crystal will benefit from being exposed to it, you should take a pair of tongs or something and quickly stick the crystal into the flame. You only need to do this for five to ten seconds, as the cleansing properties of fire are quick to take effect and destroy the impurities.

Another fairly standard way of cleansing a crystal is to use saltwater. Salt has been used in magic rituals throughout history, and it has a very purging effect on negative energy. There is a reason why people would throw a handful of salt over their shoulders to ward off bad luck. Crystals should be left in a saltwater mixture overnight. Use sea salt rather than the kind you put on your french fries. If you have an ocean nearby, you can leave them in the water overnight for the best results. Just make sure that you use a bag or some other means of preventing them from being washed out to sea. As with rainwater, there are some crystals that don't benefit from this method as the salt can damage them. Plus, there are crystals that dissolve in water or change their structure, so always make sure you research the best method of cleansing any particular crystal before you embark on the ritual.

**Be Willing to Experiment**

Throughout this book, we have discussed many different crystals and many different ways of using them. I have recommended crystals that are suitable for beginners and have talked you through cleansing them. But none of this should be considered the end of the road when it comes to learning and experimenting with them. We are dealing with energy here, and the one thing that is a constant when it comes to energy is that the individual's relationship with that energy is unique and fertile. If you have reached this far in the book, you might think that you know everything you need to know about crystals. While you know everything you need to get started using them, no book, no matter how long it is, could fully cover the unique and malleable features of working with energy or crystals. To fully align with your crystals, you need to open yourself up and be ready to experiment.

We see this most clearly in our discussion of crystal grids. You can feel where each crystal needs to be placed, but what you feel is not going to be the same as what your best friend feels or what I feel. If we each had the same crystals, we would still walk away with a unique grid that reflects us personally. That is because nobody has the same energy as another person. So, instead of following everything that is written about crystals, you need to stay open. Try new things. Try combinations that you haven't seen people talk about. See if you can't figure out a new way to use your crystals, such as creating three-dimensional grids or infusing them directly into your work. Maybe you find that rolling a crystal is a more effective way of making a choice than rolling a dice. Perhaps you are an artist, and you find that using crystals to help you select colors or even to paint turns out to be beneficial. There are endless possibilities, so long as you are willing to experiment.

## Chapter Summary

- Despite the fact that we should be cautious when we're a beginner, we shouldn't avoid powerful stones if they call to us.

- If you are buying your crystals online, stick to the ones for beginners as you won't be able to judge how the stronger ones make you feel.

- Before going into the store to purchase crystals, take a moment to meditate. A few deep breaths are all that is needed. You may want to tell yourself that you aren't powerful, so as to quiet down the ego.

- In the store, look at each of the crystals available and let yourself be drawn in naturally to any that call out to you.

- You should cleanse your crystals immediately after buying them.

- While you may want to jump into the deep end and make crystal grids with dozens of different types, you should start with a single crystal and then slowly work your way up from there.

- Being overwhelmed by the energy of your crystals can cause anxiety and feelings of not belonging. That could be the equivalent of blowing a fuse and it might really mess with your chakras.

- Crystals should be cleansed after they are purchased, before being used to make crystal elixirs, and at least once a month at the minimum.

- The easiest way to cleanse a crystal is to use natural water, such as leaving it outside in the rain for five to ten minutes.

- Sunlight can be used to cleanse a crystal, but light from the full moon is far more powerful and effective.

- Earth crystals can be buried in the ground for 24 hours as a way of cleansing.

- Fire crystals can be cleansed by being put in flame for five seconds.

- Saltwater will also work to purify crystals. Crystals should be placed in saltwater overnight; just make sure your crystals aren't the kind that are damaged by salt.

- While everything in this book has been to help you get started, you should be ready to toss it all out and go with your gut. Listen to your crystals.

- Be willing to experiment and try new things with your crystals.

# FINAL WORDS

As the book comes to a close, we approach the end of our time together. It has been my hope that I was able to give you a better understanding of these powerful tools. While they are called healing crystals, it should be clear by now, this doesn't mean they replace medical care. These crystals can serve to help us heal physically, but they are most concerned with our emotional, mental, and spiritual well-being.

This is important; our emotional and spiritual health is highly threatened in our 21st-century culture. We are expected to work longer hours, to push ourselves to achieve more, and yet we are also supposed to keep up with the news and stay active on social media or be reachable by texts at all hours of the day. It's a way of life that creates a lot of pressure on us, demands that aren't normal for the human animal. We have developed over centuries to get to where we are, but we have forgotten how important it is to keep our spiritual and psychological health in check. We often come unaligned from our deepest self, and this causes us a lot of pain.

Healing crystals are one of the many ways we can use to help us to repair this damage. We saw in chapter one that these crystals are used for many different purposes, though almost all of them had one thing in common:

they are used for healing some aspect of ourselves. It could be letting go of pain, learning to relax, warding off negative energy and inviting positivity, or accessing other elements of our potential.

It's vital not to ignore the emotional side of our existence, yet we so often do. We might be having issues relaxing, letting go of stress and anxiety, or even finding our happiness. Chapter two showed us how many different crystals can be used to achieve whatever emotional effect we are after. But not every crystal is suitable for beginners. That's why we looked at those crystals with a subtle energy in chapter three. If you are ordering your crystals online, then you should stick to those crystals we discussed in that chapter.

Crystals can be used as jewelry, as part of meditation, or even to infuse our water with their healing properties. Chapter four looked at the many ways that we might want to use crystals. Chapter five then looked at how we can maximize our experience with these crystals to have the most beneficial and positive time possible. One of the key points here was to open up and be willing to experiment. You shouldn't only rely on what we talked about in chapter four, but be adventurous in finding new ways of using your crystals.

Remember that no matter what you hear or what people say, the relationship that you have to your crystals will be the clearest way to define what is right and wrong. If you are drawn to a powerful crystal, it could be that you have an energy that matches it appropriately. Likewise, you should be willing to explore new ways of benefiting from your relationship with your crystals. If you approach them with this mindset, you will have a much easier and enjoyable experience working with them as they bring positive energy into your life.

www.ingramcontent.com/pod-product-compliance
Lightning Source LLC
Chambersburg PA
CBHW050323120526
44592CB00014B/2027